CREATIVE CROCKERY COOKING

Ethel Lang Graham

WEATHERVANE
BOOKS

Contents

Introduction

Beans, soups, dried fruits, and inexpensive, less-tender cuts of meat are delicious when prepared in a slow cooker. Such dishes are hearty, substantial, and best-prepared early in the day and practically ignored until moments before dinner is to be served. In fact, it's best not to peek under the lid during long, slow cooking, because each peek releases heat. This marvelous appliance is handy indeed for a working homemaker or someone who comes home ravenous and ready for hearty fare instantly.

Soups and dried beans are so good when prepared in the slow cooker, you'll undoubtedly make some of these recipes a regular part of your daily menus. Do be sure to prepare hot oatmeal for breakfast on the next chilly evening.

In these energy-conscious times, the slow cooker should prove to be an inexpensive energy-saving appliance. Check the watts used by your slow cooker, your electric surface units, and your electric oven. You undoubtedly will find the slow cooker, even though it may operate for 8 or 9 hours at a time, uses fewer total watt-hours of energy. Energy-saving is usually greatest whenever the slow cooker can be used in place of an oven for baked products, pot roasts, scrumptious granolas, and custards.

Recipes in this book were developed and tested with Rival model 3100 3½-quart Crock Pots. These have heating coils in the sides only, nonremovable crockery liners, and they operate on 75 watts of power on low heat and 150 watts on the high-heat setting. Should you already own a larger, 5-quart slow cooker, merely increase the recipes by half in order to keep cooking times comparable. Otherwise, cooking times may need to be decreased somewhat because of the higher wattage of the larger cookers.

Some slow cookers have heating coils only in the bottom. Recipes in this book were not developed for this type of cooker. More evaporation occurs during cooking, and baking is unsatisfactory in them.

My family and friends were chief tasters and critics during the development of these recipes. You'll find many of their thoughts and preferences noted in the recipe introductions. Recipes for foods judged to taste better when prepared quickly in a saucepan or baked in an oven have been omitted. Good taste was always our most important consideration.

Many of my students have asked about the nutritive value of slow-cooked foods. Unfortunately, no large-scale study has been conducted to date in this area. Long cooking, even at temperatures below the boiling point, may partially destroy some vitamins, especially those in vegetables. Some of this loss may be avoided by adding the succulent ones during the last 10 or 15 minutes of cooking, as I have suggested. Better color and interesting texture-retention are also advantages of brief cooking.

Water-soluble vitamins and mineral salts partially dissolve out of foods into the surrounding cooking liquid. Fats melt out of meats and float to the surface. Skim off accumulated fat, which is largely saturated, and be sure to consume the cooking liquids as a sauce or gravy.

selection and uses of a slow cooker

Two main types of slow cookers are available. One type has heating coils in the sides; the other is heated from the base. By all means, select one from among those with side-coil heating. Heat distribution is more uniform and less evaporation occurs during cooking. This type also can be used for baking and for casserole-type dishes.

Most homemakers do not wash the crockery liner in the dishwasher because it takes up so much space. The intact cooker is easily cleaned in the sink. A removable crockery liner costs more and may not be a highly important feature in a slow cooker.

A removable cord may be an advantage during cleaning and may enable the slow cooker to be used at the table as a server.

Several sizes of cookers are available. The 3½-quart size seems to be most popular for families of 4 to 6 persons. Recipes given here are for the 3½-quart cooker. Ingredients may be increased by half for a 5-quart cooker and larger-size roasts may be purchased.

Most slow cookers have two heat selections. In a 3½-quart cooker, low heat uses about 75 watts and keeps liquids 20 to 30°F below the boiling point if the temperature is measured in the center of a full cooker. High heat uses approximately 150 watts and causes liquids to boil very slowly. Generally, foods cooked on high heat cook twice as rapidly as those cooked on low. High heat must be used for baked goods and steamed puddings.

In most recipes for meats and vegetables, the time on low heat is given. If you wish a more speedy preparation, turn the heat to high and reduce the cooking time by half. To shorten cooking times slightly, turn the heat to high for the last hour or two.

uses of a slow cooker

Pot roasts

Cuts most suitable for pot-roasting in a 3½-quart slow cooker are 2 to 3 pound beef chuck, rump, or the bottom of the round roasts. These are flavorful and reasonably priced. Small roasts of pork, lamb, and veal are also suitable.

Liquids may not have to be added to pot roasts. One to 2 cups of liquid usually form in the slow cooker during cooking.

Some browning of the exterior of the roast occurs during cooking where the meat protrudes from the cooking liquid. Pre-browning of the roast in a skillet may not be necessary for the development of a good, meaty flavor.

Gravy is prepared after cooking by pouring accumulated liquids into a saucepan, skimming off fat, and thickening with a flour-and-water paste. If sufficient tomato paste is used, it will thicken the gravy during cooking, and no last-minute thickening will be necessary.

Stews

Less expensive lean cuts of meat should be selected for stewing. Those suitable for pot-roasting are ideal. Trim away fat and cube the meat. Always *brown* cubed meats for stews in a large skillet. Pour off accumulated fat to reduce the caloric value and saturated-fat content of the dish. The browned bits in the skillet must be picked up with a little liquid and added to the slow cooker with the meat. If browning is not done, the gravy will not be brown, and the stew will have an insipid flavor. In fact, you may never try it again.

Gravy may be prepared either before or after the meat has slow-cooked. To prepare gravy after the stew has cooked, pour the accumulated liquid into a saucepan, thicken it with a flour-and-water paste, and return it to the stew.

If you do not wish to have any last-minute preparation or are leaving the stew for someone else to eat, the gravy may be thickened prior to cooking. Place the browned meat in the slow cooker, drain off accumulated fat, add the recipe liquid to the skillet, and thicken it with a flour-and-water paste. Add it to the meat and vegetables in the slow cooker. The gravy must be very thick at this stage, because additional liquids will accumulate and cause it to become thinner during cooking.

Gravies for stews and pot roasts

The proportions of flour and water used to thicken accumulated cooking liquids vary with your preferences. Usually 2 to 3 tablespoons of flour mixed until lump-free in a shaker jar with 2 to 3 tablespoons of cold water per each cup of accumulated cooking liquid produces the best results. More or less of this flour-and-water paste may be used, according to your preferences.

Flour will not thicken gravy properly unless the gravy is stirred and boiled for a minute or 2. It certainly seems more convenient to do this in a saucepan rather than in the slow cooker (even if one more pan is necessary). It may take 30 minutes for a slow cooker to bring cooking liquids to a boil when the heat setting is turned from low to high. Meanwhile, if the meat is removed it becomes cold.

Do not thicken gravies with tapioca rather than flour. This has been recommended because tapioca starch will thicken gravy on low heat, just below the boiling point. Your family, your guests, and you may not like the texture of tapioca-thickened gravies. If you wish to try it, use half the amount of tapioca than the amount of flour you usually use. Add it the last 30 to 60 minutes of cooking.

Vegetables in stews and pot roasts

Most vegetables require at least 8 hours of cooking on low heat to soften. They cook more evenly when placed underneath a pot roast where liquid accumulates or when covered with a stew's liquid ingredients. For stews and pot roasts, root vegetables should be cut into 1-inch pieces. Smaller pieces or thin slices may disintegrate during long cooking.

Green vegetables cannot be cooked satisfactorily for long periods of time in the slow cooker. These vegetables are best when heated only until tender. Long cooking converts their green chlorophyll to an olive-green pigment. They lose their crisp texture and no longer contribute color to the dish.

For best results add green vegetables during the last 10 to 30 minutes of cooking. Frozen, defrosted vegetables such as green beans, peas, and limas are especially suitable. Stir them into stews during the last 5 or 10 minutes of cooking. Freezing and blanching have softened them. Defrosting speeds cooking by preventing them from chilling the stew excessively. Cooking is more uniform.

Fresh, sliced green peppers in season also can be used to add color and a crisp texture to stews. Add these the last 5 or 10 minutes of cooking.

Onions and garlic do not need browning or softening in oil. Add these along with other vegetables prior to cooking.

Beans

Dried beans are a natural for the slow cooker. The long cooking seems to break down the compound found under the skins of beans that is responsible for intestinal gas.

Beans are inexpensive and nourishing. One cup of most cooked beans furnishes as much total protein as 3 ounces of cooked meat. If beans are served with a generous portion of a grain product, their protein is made nearly comparable in quality to that of meat.

With the exception of lentils and split peas, all dried beans must be rehydrated prior to cooking. Lentils and split peas successfully rehydrate during cooking without unnecessarily prolonging cooking times.

Either of two methods may be used for rehydration. Either soak beans in the recipe water for 4 to 8 hours or add the recipe water to the beans, boil them for 2 minutes, and let them soak in this water for 1 hour.

Beans must be cooked in their soaking liquid (to conserve nutrients) for 2 to 3 hours on high heat to cook and soften their starch. No amount of cooking on low heat or below the boiling point will soften them.

After beans are tender, the cooking liquid is reserved, and other more flavorful liquids are added. Only enough reserved cooking liquid is returned to the beans to barely cover them. Excess liquids make the beans watery because little evaporation occurs during cooking. Beans are then cooked on low heat for 8 to 12 hours so that the flavor of all those luscious ingredients will penetrate the otherwise flavorless beans.

Molasses, brown sugar, tomato sauce, catsup, or vinegar are added to beans only after they have been softened on high heat. Molasses contains calcium, and the other ingredients are acidic. All harden beans and prolong cooking time. Salt or salted ham may be added to beans after soaking and before cooking if the beans are only to be softened and no long cooking is to be done.

Cheese, if used, is added the last 15 to 20 minutes of cooking. Long cooking will cause it to separate.

Canned beans may be substituted for cooked dried beans in some recipes. One pound (2 cups) dried beans yields 4 to 5 cups cooked beans. The drained canned beans may be combined with recipe-flavoring ingredients and cooked on low heat as the recipe directs. Canned beans cost more, but soaking and cooking on high for 2 to 3 hours are eliminated.

Bean soups are prepared in exactly the same manner as bean dishes except more liquids are added. Smoked, salted ham may be added either prior to cooking on high or prior to cooking on low.

Soups

The slow cooker is excellent to use for preparation of meat soups or meat stock. Slow-cooked bean soups may well be among the best you have prepared.

Rice and noodles must be cooked according to package directions and added to soups a few minutes before serving. These disintegrate with long cooking. Converted rice or barley may be added prior to cooking or 3 to 4 hours before the end of cooking. These tolerate long cooking.

Milk or cream soups are not suitable for the slow cooker. Milk products curdle on long cooking. Sour cream, milk, or cream must be stirred in just before serving and heated only briefly.

Sauces

Sauces are probably most successfully cooked only 3 to 4 hours on low heat to blend flavors. Long cooking tends to diminish the flavor of spices and herbs. If long cooking is desired, add spices and herbs about 20 minutes before serving the dish.

Spices and herbs

The flavors of dried herbs and ground spices do not tolerate long cooking. Either use more or add them the last 30 to 60 minutes of cooking. Whole spices — cinnamon sticks, whole cloves, black peppercorns — are far more preferable.

Rice

Converted rice must be used in slow-cooked recipes. It will soften successfully with little disintegration. Whole-grain and regular rice require *high* heat for at least 1½ hours to soften. Converted rice has been partially steamed prior to milling. This is done to force nutrients into the endosperm before the bran and germ are milled away. Long cooking decomposes the instant rices.

Oatmeal

Old-fashioned oats, not quick-cooking oats, must be used when preparing oatmeal in the slow cooker. Quick-cooking oats are rolled thinner and tend to disintegrate with overnight heating on low. Obviously, there is no purpose in using instant oatmeal in a slow cooker.

Milk products

Milk and creams curdle with long cooking and are always added just before serving.

10

Pork

Most slow-cooked dishes reach the necessary temperature of 150°F necessary to prevent trichinosis from consuming improperly cooked, infected pork.

Fish

Seafood should be cooked for short periods of time. Cooking methods other than slow-cooking are far better. Only a few fish recipes have been included here.

Other tips

Don't lift the lid off the slow cooker during cooking. Each peek results in heat loss. Do not peek when baking. Begin testing baked products for doneness only after 2 hours of baking or at the minimum time in the cooking range given in the recipe.

Avoid rapid temperature changes which may crack the crockery lining.

Use only plastic scouring pads to remove stubborn stains. Other materials may scratch the lining.

other uses of the slow cooker

As a casserole dish

The slow cooker can be used to prepare most casserole-type dishes. It will usually use less electricity than an oven and be less likely to heat your kitchen on a hot day.

Assemble the casserole ingredients in the slow cooker. Cover and cook on high. In about an hour a dish to serve 4 will be heated through. The top-surface browning is a little less than when baked in an oven.

Our favorites are the Enchiladas, Manicotti, Lasagna, Pizza Beans, and Italian Bean and Cheese Casserole of the recipes prepared in this manner.

As a baker

With a suitable mold the slow cooker can be used as an oven. High heat for 2 to 3 hours is necessary for most oven-type dishes.

Some suggested molds for baking in a 3½-quart slow cooker follow.

1) A 3-pound hydrogenated shortening can fits perfectly inside the slow cooker and holds 7 to 8 cups.

2) A 48-ounce juice can or a 2-pound coffee can with the top ½ inch cut away with tin snips holds 5 cups. Left intact, the can will not fit under the lid.

3) Rival's Bread 'n Bake pan is an aluminum mold with a specially vented lid. At this writing it is available by mail directly from Rival. Write to them for information.

4) A small tube pan or souffle dish often can be found to fit inside the slow cooker.

The following are some suggested foods to bake in a slow cooker.

1) Nut breads. Those containing about 2 cups of flour fit well into a 3-pound shortening can. Cover the can loosely with aluminum foil to shield the bread from condensation.

2) Yeast breads. Those with 3 cups of flour fit well into a trimmed 48-ounce juice can and form a perfect round loaf for luncheon meats.

3) Mixes. A 16-ounce pound-cake mix or a 1-layer cake mix fit well into a Bread 'n Bake pan or a 3-pound hydrogenated shortening can.

Products baked in a mold in the slow cooker are very tender, delicate, and moist. Many crumble easily unless thoroughly cooled before slicing.

Try at least one of the baked products given in this book. Here again, the slow cooker probably uses less energy than an oven. If you prefer, each of the recipes given for breads can be baked in a 9 × 5-inch loaf pan in a 350°F oven for about 50 minutes.

As a steamer

Boston Brown Bread, steamed fruit puddings, and custards are a few of the many recipes that can be prepared by steaming in the slow cooker.

Select a proper-sized mold; fill and cover it as directed. Set the mold inside the slow cooker on a small trivet to allow for better water circulation. Add the recommended amount of boiling water. Cover and cook on high as the recipe directs. Avoid unnecessarily peeking under the lid and allowing steam to escape. The mold must be covered as directed to protect its contents from the droplets of condensed water that form inside the lid and drip onto the mold during cooking.

breakfast foods

cinnamon oatmeal and fruit

What a treat this is to come downstairs to on a chilly morning!

Yield: 4 servings

3 cups cold water
1½ cups old-fashioned oatmeal
½ teaspoon cinnamon
¼ cup raisins
1 apple, cored, peeled, and cut into ½-inch cubes
1 teaspoon salt

Combine all ingredients in the slow cooker at bedtime. Cook on low overnight, 8 to 10 hours. Serve with milk.

hot oatmeal

Try this in place of cold cereal on winter mornings.

Yield: 4 servings

1½ cups old-fashioned oatmeal (not quick oats)
3 cups cold water
1 teaspoon salt

Combine ingredients in the slow cooker at bedtime. Cook on low 8 to 10 hours or overnight. Serve hot in the morning with milk and a dash of nutmeg.

Variations
Add 1 cup grated carrots before cooking.
Add 2 or 3 tablespoons brown sugar before cooking.

hot rolled wheat

Rolled wheat makes an interesting change from oatmeal. You can find it in most natural-food stores.

Yield: 4 servings

1½ cups rolled wheat
3 cups cold water
1 teaspoon salt

Combine ingredients in the slow cooker at bedtime. Cook on low overnight, 8 to 10 hours. Serve from the pot in the morning with honey or brown sugar and milk.

crunchy granola

Make your own whole-grain granola cereal.

Yield: About 5 cups

4 cups rolled oats	¼ cup vegetable oil
⅔ cup wheat germ	⅔ cup honey
¼ cup sesame seeds	1 teaspoon vanilla
¼ cup shredded coconut	½ cup raisins

Combine all ingredients except the raisins in the slow cooker. Heat on low with lid slightly ajar for about 4 hours. Stir occasionally. Let cool and add raisins. Store in a tightly covered container. Use within 1 to 2 weeks.

honey–wheat granola

Yield: About 5 cups

1 cup rolled wheat (available from natural-food stores)	½ cup hulled sunflower seeds
3 cups rolled oats	¼ cup vegetable oil
½ cup wheat germ	1 teaspoon vanilla
½ cup honey	¼ teaspoon salt
	¼ cup chopped dried apricots or dates

Combine all ingredients except the dried fruit in the slow cooker. Cook on low with lid slightly ajar for about 4 hours, stirring occasionally. Cool, add dried fruit, and store in an airtight jar. Use within 1 to 2 weeks.

cinnamon–cocoa granola

Especially good!

Yield: 5 cups

    4 cups rolled oats
    1 cup bran flakes
    1 cup wheat germ
    2 tablespoons cocoa
    ¾ cup honey
    ¼ cup vegetable oil
    1 teaspoon cinnamon
    ½ cup sesame seeds

Combine all ingredients in the slow cooker. Cook on low heat with lid slightly ajar about 4 hours, stirring occasionally. Cool and store in airtight jars. Use within 1 to 2 weeks.

the ultimate granola

The gourmet's granola.

Yield: About 6 cups

    3 cups rolled oats
    1 cup wheat germ
    1 cup shredded coconut
    ½ cup sesame seeds
    ½ cup coarsely chopped cashews
    ½ cup coarsely chopped almonds
    ⅔ cup honey
    ¼ cup vegetable oil
    Dash cinnamon and nutmeg
    ½ cup raisins
    ½ cup chopped dates

Combine all ingredients except the raisins and dates in the slow cooker. Cook on low with lid slightly ajar for about 4 hours, stirring occasionally. Cool and add fruit. Store in airtight jars. Use within 1 to 2 weeks.

meats

beef stew

No need for last-minute thickening of the gravy with the technique used here. A good, hearty stew.

Yield: 6 servings

> 2 pounds lean beef
>   (round, chuck, sirloin tip, rump), cut into 1-inch cubes
> ⅓ cup all-purpose flour
> 2 tablespoons vegetable oil
> 4 potatoes, cut into 1-inch cubes
> 6 carrots, cut into 1-inch slices
> 1 onion, chopped
> 2 cups water
> ⅓ cup all-purpose flour in ⅓ cup cold water, mixed to a paste
> 2 teaspoons salt
> ½ cup frozen defrosted peas
> Fresh parsley leaves

Toss beef cubes in flour; shake off excess. Brown in hot oil in a large skillet for about 10 minutes.

Place meat in slow cooker with potatoes, carrots, and onion.

Drain accumulated fat from skillet. Add water, flour–water mixture, and salt to skillet. Bring to a boil, stirring constantly, until thickened. Add mixture to meat and vegetables in slow cooker. Cover and cook on low for 8 to 10 hours.

Add peas last 10 minutes of cooking to heat through. Serve hot, garnished with parsley leaves.

Variations to beef stew

To the gravy, add one of the following:

> ¼ cup tomato paste
> 1 teaspoon oregano and 1 teaspoon basil
> 1 tablespoon Worcestershire sauce or soy sauce

red-wine stew

Yield: 6 to 8 servings

3 to 4 slices bacon, cubed
2 pounds lean beef and pork, cut into
    1-inch cubes (or use all beef)
1 whole onion
4 whole cloves
3 onions, chopped
1 bay leaf
2 carrots, sliced

1½ teaspoons salt
1½ cups dry red wine
2 hot dogs
1 cup green beans, peas, or chopped
    green pepper
2 tomatoes, quartered
Fresh parsley leaves
Flour–water paste (optional)

Brown bacon in a large skillet; add beef and pork cubes and brown well on all sides.

Place meat in slow cooker along with a whole onion studded with the cloves, chopped onions, bay leaf, carrots, and salt.

Pour accumulated fat from skillet and add some of the red wine. Stir to pick up the browned bits.

Add to slow cooker along with remaining wine. Cover and cook on low about 8 hours.

Add hot dogs the last ½ hour and the green vegetable and tomatoes the last 10 minutes of cooking.

Before serving, remove whole onion and cloves. Garnish with parsley.

Gravy may be thickened in a saucepan with a flour–water paste if desired.

red-wine stew

beef stew with apples and white wine

Yield: 6 servings

2½ pounds lean beef,
    cut into 1-inch cubes
2 tablespoons vegetable
    oil or olive oil
2 cloves garlic
2 carrots, cut into 1-inch cubes
2 onions, cut into wedges

1 teaspoon salt
¾ cup dry white wine
¾ cup apple cider
2 apples, peeled, cored, and cut into
    1-inch cubes
¼ cup all-purpose flour in ¼ cup
    cold water, mixed to a paste

Brown beef in hot oil in a large skillet.

Place meat in slow cooker with garlic, carrots, onions, salt, and wine.

Add the cider to the skillet and stir to pick up the browned bits.

Add cider to slow cooker. Cover and cook on low about 8 hours. Add apples the last 3 hours of cooking.

Pour accumulated juice into a saucepan. Add flour–water paste. Heat, stirring constantly, until mixture boils and is thickened.

Return mixture to meat and vegetables. Serve at once.

sailor's stew

Yield: 6 servings

4 slices bacon, cubed
2 to 2½ pounds lean beef
  (chuck, round, rump),
  cut into ½-inch slices
4 potatoes, sliced
3 dill pickles, sliced

3 onions, sliced
Salt and pepper
1 bay leaf
1 cup beef bouillon
Flour–water paste (optional)

Fry bacon in a large skillet until transparent. Remove bacon and set aside. Brown beef slices in hot bacon fat about 1 minute per side.

Arrange beef slices, potato slices, pickle slices, onion slices, and cooked bacon in slow cooker in alternate layers. Season each layer lightly with salt and pepper. Add beef bouillon and bay leaf. Cover and cook on low about 8 hours. Serve piping hot.

Accumulated cooking liquid may be thickened in a saucepan with a flour–water paste, if desired.

sailor's stew

hungarian kettle stew

Yield: 4 servings

1 pound lean beef,
    cut into 1-inch cubes
2 tablespoons vegetable
    oil or bacon fat
1½ cups water
2 medium onions, chopped
1 clove garlic, minced
4 potatoes, cut into 1-inch cubes
1 teaspoon salt
1 tablespoon tomato paste

1 tablespoon paprika
1 teaspoon caraway seeds
2 tomatoes, coarsely chopped
2 green peppers, cubed
3 tablespoons all-purpose flour
    in 3 tablespoons
    cold water, mixed to a paste
½ cup sour cream
Parsley for garnish (optional)

Brown beef in hot oil in a large skillet. Place in slow cooker.

Pour off accumulated fat. Add some of the water to the skillet and stir to pick up the browned bits. Add to the meat along with remaining water, onions, garlic, potatoes, salt, tomato paste, paprika, and caraway seeds. Cover and cook on low about 8 hours.

Add tomatoes and green peppers the last 5 minutes of cooking.

Pour accumulated gravy into a saucepan, add flour–water mixture, and bring to a boil, stirring constantly, until thickened. Stir in sour cream and return mixture at once to meat and vegetables. Serve immediately in hot bowls. Garnish with parsley leaves, if you wish.

hungarian kettle stew

panamanian stew

You can substitute a 1½-pound round steak, cut into ½-inch strips, for the pork and beef.

Yield: 4 to 6 servings

    1 pound lean beef, cut into ¾-inch cubes
    8 ounces lean pork, cut into ¾-inch cubes
    2 tablespoons vegetable oil or bacon fat
    3 cups water
    2 carrots, sliced into ¼-inch slices
    1 beet, peeled and cut into ½-inch cubes
    2 stalks celery, cut into ¾-inch slices
    2 medium potatoes, cut into ¾-inch cubes
    2 onions, sliced
    ½ small head cabbage, shredded
    2 teaspoons salt
    2 tomatoes, peeled and quartered
    1 cup frozen, defrosted green beans
    2 tablespoons fresh parsley leaves, chopped
    ½ teaspoon basil or thyme

Brown beef and pork in oil in a large skillet. Place meat in slow cooker.

Add some of the water to the skillet and stir to pick up the browned bits. Add to the meat along with remaining water, carrots, beet, celery, potatoes, onions, cabbage, and salt. Cover and cook on low about 8 hours or until vegetables are tender.

Add tomatoes, green beans, parsley, and basil the last 10 minutes of cooking. Serve stew hot in large bowls with crusty Italian rolls.

red-stewed beef

Red-stewing is the Chinese method of preparing less-tender cuts of meat.

Yield: 6 servings

    3 pounds lean pot roast (chuck, round, rump, or sirloin tip)
    ½ cup soy sauce
    ¼ cup sherry
    4 slices fresh gingerroot
    3 scallions
    1 clove garlic
    2 tablespoons brown sugar
    ½ teaspoon anise seeds
    1 cup water

Place pot roast in slow cooker and add remaining ingredients. Cover and cook on low about 10 hours. Slice meat and cover with cooking sauce as it is served.

Picture on previous pages: panamanian stew

beef paprika

Lamb may be substituted for beef in this recipe with excellent results. A very good dish.

Yield: 6 servings

2 to 3 pounds lean beef,
    cut into 1-inch cubes
2 tablespoons bacon fat or
    vegetable oil
2 to 3 tablespoons water
1 6-ounce can tomato paste

2 cloves garlic
1½ tablespoons paprika
1 teaspoon salt
2 green peppers, cut into 1-inch strips
1 cup sour cream

Brown beef in hot fat in a large skillet. Place meat in slow cooker.

Pour off accumulated fat and add water to skillet. Stir to pick up browned bits. Add to meat along with tomato paste, garlic, paprika, and salt. Cover and cook on low about 8 hours. Add green peppers the last 10 minutes of cooking.

Just before serving, lightly fold in the sour cream. It need not be uniformly distributed. Serve immediately.

beef paprika

carbonnade of beef 'n beer

This recipe requires the use of the oven.

Yield: 6 servings

2 to 3 pounds lean beef,
    cut into 1-inch cubes
2 tablespoons vegetable oil
3 onions, sliced
2 cloves garlic
12 black peppercorns
1 bay leaf
1 teaspoon thyme

1½ teaspoons salt
1 tablespoon sugar
1 12-ounce can beer
4 tablespoons all-purpose flour in
    4 tablespoons cold water, mixed
    to a smooth paste
6 thin slices bread
French mustard

Brown beef in hot oil in a skillet. Place in slow cooker with onions, garlic, peppercorns, bay leaf, thyme, salt, and sugar.

Drain fat from skillet and add beer and the flour–water paste. Heat and stir until mixture comes to a boil and is thickened. Add to slow cooker. Cover and cook on low 8 to 10 hours.

Pour stew into a shallow casserole dish. Spread each slice of bread with mustard. Place the slices mustard-side-down over the stew. Press to imbed lightly in gravy. Place in 350° F oven 15 to 20 minutes to brown the bread. Serve at once.

budapest gulyasuppe

Yield: 4 servings

1 pound lean beef,
    cut into 1-inch cubes
2 tablespoons vegetable oil
    or bacon fat
1½ cups water
½ cup dry red wine
4 potatoes, cut into 1-inch cubes
2 onions, chopped
2 cloves garlic
1 teaspoon salt

¼ teaspoon pepper
1 tablespoon paprika
Dash Tabasco sauce
2 tomatoes, peeled and cubed
2 green peppers, cubed
1 teaspoon marjoram
3 tablepoons all-purpose flour in
    3 tablespoons cold water, mixed to
    a paste (optional)

Brown the beef in hot oil in a large skillet. Place meat in slow cooker.

Pour off accumulated fat and add some of the water to the skillet. Stir to pick up the browned bits. Pour into the slow cooker. Add remaining water, wine, potatoes, onions, garlic, salt, pepper, paprika, and Tabasco sauce. Cover and cook on low about 8 hours.

Add tomatoes, green peppers, and marjoram during the last 5 to 10 minutes of cooking.

If a thickened gravy is desired, pour juice into a saucepan, add flour-water mixture, and bring to a boil, stirring constantly, until thickened. Return gravy to meat and vegetables.

Picture on opposite page: budapest gulyasuppe

marie's quick onion pot roast

This roast needs no prior browning. Meat browns in slow cooker and forms a brown gravy. Prepare vegetables separately so flavor and textures in this meal are distinct.

Yield: 6 to 8 servings

> 1 envelope onion-soup mix
> 3 pounds lean beef pot roast (chuck or round), fat trimmed away
> 3 tablespoons all-purpose flour in 3 tablespoons cold water, mixed to a paste

Sprinkle onion-soup mix over the bottom of the slow cooker. Add pot roast. Cover and cook on low about 10 hours or on high about 5 hours.

Pour accumulated juices into a saucepan; skim off fat. Add flour–water paste and bring to a boil, stirring constantly until thickened. Serve over sliced meat.

i-can't-believe-it's-so-easy pot roast

Surface of meat will brown while the meat cooks.

Yield: 6 servings

> 4 potatoes, cut into 1-inch cubes
> 8 carrots, cut into 1-inch slices
> 1 onion, chopped
> 3 pounds lean beef pot roast (chuck, round, rump)
> 1 teaspoon salt
> ½ teaspoon pepper
> 3 tablespoons all-purpose flour in 3 tablespoons cold water, mixed to a paste

Place vegetables in bottom of the slow cooker. Season meat with salt and pepper. Place on top of vegetables. Cook on low 10 to 12 hours.

Pour accumulated juice into a saucepan; skim off fat. Add flour–water mixture. Bring to a boil, stirring constantly until thickened. Return to meat and vegetables. Serve at once.

barbecued pot roast

Yield: 6 servings

     1 teaspoon salt
     2 pounds lean beef pot roast (rump, round, or chuck)
     ½ cup tomato paste
     24 peppercorns
     1 small onion, chopped
     1 teaspoon Worcestershire sauce

Sprinkle salt over pot roast and place in slow cooker. Spread tomato paste over meat; imbed peppercorns in paste; top with onions and Worcestershire sauce. Cover and cook on low 8 to 10 hours. Serve meat with accumulated gravy.

garofaloto
(italian pot roast)

Yield: 6 to 8 servings

     3 pounds lean beef pot roast (chuck, rump, or round)
     3 to 4 tablespoons olive oil
     12 whole cloves
     ¼ teaspoon freshly ground black pepper
     3 cloves garlic
     1 cup Chianti wine
     ½ cup tomato paste
     1½ teaspoons salt
     1 tablespoon sugar

Brown beef on all sides in hot olive oil in a large skillet. Place in slow cooker. Insert whole cloves in the top of the beef. Sprinkle with pepper. Poke holes in the lean portions and fill holes with olive oil.

Combine remaining ingredients and pour around beef. Cover and cook on low 8 to 10 hours. Remove meat and keep it warm.

Strain the accumulated juice into a saucepan. Skim off fat. Boil rapidly until juice is reduced by half. Slice meat and spoon juice over it as it is served.

poppy-seed pot roast with sour-cream gravy

Yield: 6 to 8 servings

3 pounds lean beef pot roast
    (chuck, rump, or round)
2 tablespoons vegetable oil
12 small onions
6 carrots, cut into 1-inch slices

½ cup water
2 teaspoons poppy seeds
1½ teaspoons salt
Freshly ground black pepper

Brown meat on all sides in hot oil in a large skillet.

Place onions and carrots in slow cooker and place browned meat on top.

Add water to skillet and stir to pick up browned bits. Add to slow cooker along with poppy seeds, salt, and pepper. Cover and cook on low about 10 hours.

sour-cream gravy

Juices from pot roast
3 tablespoons flour in 3 tablespoons cold water, mixed to a paste
1 teaspoon paprika
½ cup sour cream

Pour accumulated juices into a saucepan. Add flour–water paste and paprika. Bring to a boil, stirring constantly until thickened. Remove from heat and add sour cream. Serve with meat and vegetables.

zesty beef pot roast with red wine

Yield: 6 servings

2 pounds very lean beef pot roast
    (rump, round, or sirloin tip)
¼ cup all-purpose flour
2 tablespoons vegetable oil
¼ cup water
1 cup dry red wine

¼ cup all-purpose flour in ¼ cup cold
    water, mixed to a paste
1 teaspoon salt
3 bay leaves
1 dozen whole black peppercorns
1 lemon, sliced

Dredge beef with flour and brown in hot oil in a large skillet. Remove, cut into thick slices, and place in slow cooker.

Drain accumulated fat from skillet and add water. Stir to loosen browned bits. Add wine, flour–water mixture, and salt. Bring to a boil, stirring constantly until thickened. Pour over meat in the slow cooker and add remaining ingredients. Cover and cook on low 8 to 10 hours. Serve with boiled potatoes.

Lemon slices added the last hour of cooking will retain their shape and color.

Picture on opposite page: zesty beef pot roast with red wine

marinated beef pot roast

Yield: 6 servings

marinade

> 1 cup tomato juice
> 3 tablespoons prepared mustard
> 4 tablespoons Worcestershire sauce
> 1 teaspoon basil
> 1 teaspoon oregano
> 1 teaspoon onion powder
> 1 teaspoon garlic salt
> ¼ teaspoon freshly ground black pepper
>
> 3 pounds lean beef pot roast (chuck or round)
> 2 tablespoons bacon fat or vegetable oil
> Flour-water paste (optional)

Combine marinade ingredients and pour over pot roast in a shallow bowl. Cover and refrigerate overnight or for 24 hours. Remove meat from marinade and pat with paper towels to dry.

Heat bacon fat in large skillet and brown meat on all sides. Place in slow cooker. Cover and cook on low 8 to 10 hours. Serve with accumulated gravy. (This may be thickened in a saucepan with a flour-water paste if you wish.)

beef short ribs with spiced fruit

Yield: 6 servings

> 3 pounds beef short ribs
> 2 cups water
> 2 teaspoons salt
> ⅛ teaspoon pepper
> 1 11-ounce package mixed dried fruit
> ¼ cup sugar
> 1 stick cinnamon
> 2 tablespoons lemon juice

Brown short ribs in a large skillet. Drain away accumulated fat. Place meat in slow cooker. Add remaining ingredients. Cover and cook on low about 8 hours. Serve meat with fruit and accumulated juices.

sauerbraten with raisin sauce

Yield: 6 to 8 servings

marinade

> 1 cup vinegar
> 1 cup water
> 1 bay leaf
> 6 black peppercorns
> ½ teaspoon mustard seeds
> 1 medium onion, thinly sliced
>
> 3 pounds lean beef pot roast
>   (bottom of the round)
> 2 tablespoons vegetable oil
> 2 tablespoons dry red wine

sauerbraten with raisin sauce

In a large glass bowl combine marinade ingredients. Add meat, cover, and refrigerate for 3 days. Turn meat in marinade occasionally.

After 3 days remove meat. Strain and reserve marinade. Brown meat in oil in a large skillet and place in slow cooker.

Add wine and ¼ cup of the reserved marinade to the skillet and stir to pick up the browned bits. Add to meat. Cover and cook on low 8 to 10 hours.

raisin sauce

> 2 ounces crushed ginger snaps
> 2 tablespoons all-purpose flour in
>   2 tablespoons cold water,
>   mixed to a paste
> ⅓ cup raisins
> ¼ cup heavy cream or sour cream (optional)
> Salt to taste

Pour accumulated juices into a saucepan; skim off fat. Add crushed ginger snaps, flour–water mixture, and raisins. Bring to a boil, stirring constantly until thickened. Add cream if you wish. Add salt to taste. Serve gravy over hot, sliced beef.

german sauerbraten

german sauerbraten

Yield: 8 servings

3 pounds lean beef (bottom of the round)

marinade

1 cup dry red wine
½ cup red wine vinegar
1 cup water
1 medium onion, thinly sliced
1 bay leaf
3 whole cloves
6 whole black peppercorns

3 tablespoons vegetable oil or bacon fat
2 onions, chopped
1 stalk celery, chopped
1 carrot, chopped
1 teaspoon salt

gravy

> **3 tablespoons all-purpose flour in 3 tablespoons cold water, mixed to a paste**
> **Salt and pepper**
> **½ cup light or heavy cream (optional)**

Place meat in a glass bowl. Combine all marinade ingredients in a saucepan. Bring to a boil, remove from heat, and allow to cool. Pour over meat. Cover and refrigerate for 2 days. Turn meat occasionally in the marinade.

Remove meat from marinade. Strain marinade and reserve 1 cup. Brown meat on all sides in hot oil in a skillet. Place in slow cooker.

Add some of the marinade to the skillet and stir to pick up the browned bits. Add to the slow cooker along with remaining marinade, onions, celery, carrot, and salt. Cover and cook on low about 10 hours. Remove meat, slice, and keep it warm.

Strain cooking liquid into a saucepan. Add flour–water paste. Bring to a boil, stirring constantly until thickened. Season with salt and pepper. Stir in cream if desired. Pour some of the gravy over the meat. Serve remainder separately.

italian meat loaf

A favorite of my family. Good in sandwiches.

Yield: 4 servings

meat loaf

> **1 pound extra-lean ground beef**
> **2 slices rye bread, torn into soft crumbs**
> **1 onion, chopped**
> **2 tablespoons chopped fresh parsley leaves**
> **¼ cup grated Parmesan cheese**
> **1 egg**
> **1 teaspoon salt**
> **½ teaspoon freshly ground black pepper**

gravy

> **1 8-ounce can tomato sauce**
> **1 teaspoon oregano**
> **Garlic salt to taste**

Combine ingredients for meat loaf and gently form into a round loaf. Place in slow cooker on a trivet or small rack. Cover and cook on low 6 to 8 hours.

Serve with gravy prepared by combining and heating gravy ingredients in a saucepan.

dave's meat loaf

Yield: 6 servings

> 1 pound extra-lean ground beef
> ¼ pound sausage meat
> ¼ cup dark beer
> 1 egg
> 2 slices bread, torn into soft crumbs
> 1 onion, chopped
> 3 tablespoons chopped fresh parsley leaves
> 1½ teaspoons salt
> ½ teaspoon freshly ground black pepper
> Few drops Worcestershire sauce and Tabasco sauce

Combine all ingredients and gently shape into a round loaf. Place on a trivet in slow cooker. Cover and cook on low about 7 to 8 hours. Loaf should be well-done because it contains pork.

Serve with catsup or bottled chili sauce. Chill leftovers and slice for sandwiches the next day.

mexican chili con carne

Yield: 4 servings

> ½ pound kidney beans
> 4 cups water
> 1 pound lean beef or veal, cut into 1-inch cubes
> 2 tablespoons vegetable oil or bacon fat
> 1 16-ounce can tomatoes or 2 fresh tomatoes, peeled and cubed
> 1 teaspoon salt
> 1½ tablespoons chili powder
> 1 tablespoon paprika

Soak beans in water in slow cooker overnight. Do not drain. Cover and cook on high 2 to 3 hours or until tender. Drain; reserve liquid.

Brown beef in oil or bacon fat and add to beans along with remaining ingredients. Add sufficient reserved liquid to barely cover beans. Cover and cook on low 8 to 10 hours. Serve with rice.

Picture on opposite page: mexican chili con carne

chili con carne

Yield: 6 servings

    1 pound ground beef, browned in a skillet
    2 15-ounce cans red kidney beans
    1 onion, chopped
    2 tablespoons chili powder
    1 teaspoon salt
    1 clove garlic, minced
    1 8-ounce can tomato sauce
    1 tablespoon vinegar

Combine ingredients in slow cooker and cook on low for 3 to 5 hours. Serve with rice.

garlic meatballs in lemon sauce

Yield: 6 servings

meatballs

    1½ pounds extra-lean ground beef
    3 slices bread, torn into soft crumbs
    4 cloves garlic, minced
    2 tablespoons fresh parsley leaves, chopped
    2 tablespoons fresh mint leaves, chopped
    1 teaspoon paprika
    1 teaspoon salt
    Pepper to taste
    2 eggs

lemon sauce

    1 8-ounce can tomato sauce
    Grated rind from 2 lemons
    ¼ cup lemon juice
    Salt and pepper to taste
    1 tablespoon fresh mint leaves, minced

Combine all ingredients for the meatballs and form into walnut-sized balls Place in slow cooker. Combine sauce ingredients and pour over meatballs. Cover and cook on low 4 to 6 hours. Serve with rice.

hearty steak roll-ups

Yield: 4 servings

filling

3 slices bacon, cooked and crumbled
1 medium onion, chopped
4 ounces fresh or canned mushrooms,
    coarsely chopped
1 tomato, peeled and chopped
2 tablespoons fresh parsley leaves, chopped
½ teaspoon salt
⅛ teaspoon pepper

steak rolls

4 4-ounce beef sandwich steaks (very thinly
    sliced beef round)
Salt and pepper
2 tablespoons vegetable oil
1 onion, chopped
2 tablespoons tomato paste
1 cup water

hearty steak roll-up

Combine filling ingredients. Place steaks on a flat surface, season lightly with salt and pepper, and place ¼ of the filling mixture on each. Roll up, jelly-roll fashion, and fasten with string. Brown rolls lightly in hot oil and place in slow cooker. Add onion, tomato paste, and water. Cover and cook on low 6 to 8 hours. Remove beef rolls to a warm platter.

gravy

2 tablespoons all-purpose flour and 2 tablespoons cold water, mixed to a
    smooth paste
½ cup heavy cream or sour cream

Pour accumulated gravy into a saucepan; add flour–water paste and bring to a boil, stirring constantly until thickened. Stir in cream and serve at once over hot beef rolls.

cabbage rolls in beer

Yield: 8 rolls; 4 servings

1 small onion, finely chopped
1 stalk celery, minced
2 tablespoons fresh parsley
    leaves, minced
1 pound extra-lean ground beef
1 cup cooked rice

½ teaspoon salt
¼ teaspoon pepper
8 large cabbage leaves, boiled
    3 to 5 minutes, stems and thick
    veins removed

sauce

¾ cup beer
¾ cup chili sauce
1 teaspoon Worcestershire sauce
½ teaspoon salt

Combine onion, celery, parsley, beef, rice, salt, and pepper. Place ⅛ of this mixture in the center of each cabbage leaf. Fold the sides in toward the center and roll tightly. Place in slow cooker.

Combine sauce ingredients and pour over rolls. Cover and cook on low 7 to 8 hours. Serve rolls with sauce ladled over each.

kay's cabbage rolls

My neighbor's favorite recipe.

Yield: 4 servings

1 large head cabbage
1 pound extra-lean ground beef
½ cup converted rice
    (you must use *converted* rice)
1 small onion, chopped
2 fresh tomatoes, chopped
1 green pepper, chopped

½ stalk celery, chopped
1 clove garlic, minced
1 teaspoon salt
½ teaspoon pepper
½ teaspoon thyme
1 cup tomato juice

Gently remove 8 large outer leaves from the head of cabbage. Bring about 2 inches of water to a boil in a large saucepan. Add the outer cabbage leaves, cover, and simmer for 3 to 5 minutes. Drain, trim away any thick veins, and lay out for filling.

Combine beef, rice, onion, tomatoes, green pepper, celery, garlic, salt, pepper, and thyme. Place ⅛ of this mixture in the center of each cabbage leaf. Fold the sides in toward the center and roll tightly.

Chop remaining cabbage and place in the bottom of the slow cooker. Season lightly with additional salt and pepper. Place rolls on top of chopped cabbage. Add tomato juice. Cover and cook on low 6 to 8 hours. Gently remove rolls and serve with the shredded cabbage and juice.

spinach rolls

Yield: 4 to 6 servings

>   1 pound extra-lean ground beef
>   3 slices bread torn into crumbs
>   2 onions, chopped
>   1 egg
>   1 teaspoon salt
>   1/8 teaspoon pepper
>   1/2 teaspoon marjoram
>   1/8 teaspoon nutmeg
>   16 to 20 large spinach leaves, boiled 2 to 3 minutes
>   1 cup beef broth
>   2 tablespoons butter or margarine

Combine beef, bread crumbs, onions, egg, and seasonings. Place 1 heaping tablespoon of this mixture on each spinach leaf. Fold ends in toward center and roll tightly. Place rolls in slow cooker. Add broth and dot with butter. Cover and cook on low 6 to 8 hours.

spinach rolls

corned beef with horseradish

Yield: 6 to 8 servings

3 pounds corned-beef brisket
2 cups water
1 bay leaf
4 whole cloves
8 black peppercorns
½ teaspoon mustard seeds
½ teaspoon thyme

horseradish roll

½ cup whipping cream, whipped
2 tablespoons horseradish

Place corned beef in slow cooker with water, herbs, and spices. Cover and cook on low 8 to 10 hours.

Combine whipped cream and horseradish. Freeze in a 2-inch roll.

When meat is done, slice it into ½-inch slices. Arrange on a hot platter with hot cubed beets, potatoes, sliced carrots, or other vegetables. Garnish with slices of the horseradish roll.

corned beef with horseradish

new england corned-beef and cabbage dinner

Yield: 6 servings

   4 carrots, cut into 1-inch slices
   4 potatoes, cut into 1-inch cubes
   1 small head cabbage, shredded
   1 onion, sliced
   3 pounds corned-beef brisket, fat trimmed away
   1 cup water

Place vegetables in slow cooker. Add beef and water. Cover and cook on low 8 to 10 hours. Remove and slice beef. Serve with vegetables.

markat left (tunisian lamb stew)

Yield: 6 servings

1½ pounds lean lamb or mutton, cut into 1-inch cubes
3 tablespoons olive oil
1 cup water
2 medium onions, cut into ¼-inch slices
1½ teaspoons salt
1 teaspoon paprika
1 teaspoon sugar
8 large white radishes (or ½ cup red radishes), sliced paper thin
2 green peppers, sliced
8 whole small tomatoes, peeled
Chopped parsley
Flour–water paste (optional)

Brown lamb in hot olive oil in a large skillet. Place in slow cooker.

Add some of the water to the skillet and stir to pick up the browned bits. Add to the meat along with the remaining water, onions, salt, paprika, and sugar. Cover and cook on low about 8 hours.

About 5 to 10 minutes before the end of cooking, turn heat to high and add radishes, green peppers, and tomatoes. Heat only until vegetables are hot. Serve at once with rice; garnish with parsley. Serve with a dry red wine.

Gravy may be thickened, if you wish, by pouring into saucepan, adding a flour–water paste, and bringing to a boil while stirring constantly.

lamb and carrot stew

Yield: 6 servings

2 pounds lean lamb
2 cups water
5 whole black peppercorns
1 whole onion
4 potatoes, cubed
1 pound carrots, cut into ½-inch slices
½ pound kohlrabi, cut into 1-inch cubes
2 teaspoons salt
½ teaspoon caraway seeds
1 leek or 3 scallions, cut into ½-inch slices
Chopped fresh parsley
Flour–water paste (optional)

Place lamb, water, peppercorns, onion, potatoes, carrots, kohlrabi, salt, and caraway seeds in slow cooker. Cover and cook on low about 10 hours.

Add leek and parsley the last ½ hour of cooking. Remove meat; cut into 1-inch cubes and return to vegetables. Serve very hot in bowls.

Gravy may be poured into a saucepan and thickened with a flour–water paste if a thickened gravy is desired. It will not, however, be brown, as meat was not browned before cooking.

lamb and carrot stew

mint sauce for lamb stews

Yield: 1⅓ cups

⅓ cup mint jelly
½ pint sour cream
Fresh mint leaves

Melt mint jelly over low heat and stir into sour cream. Place in a bowl and garnish with fresh mint leaves. Serve with slow-cooked lamb stews or pot roasts.

lemon lamb pot roast

Yield: 6 servings

3 pounds shoulder roast of lamb,
    fat trimmed away
3 tablespoons vegetable oil
1 onion, thinly sliced
1 lemon, thinly sliced
1 bay leaf
1 teaspoon salt

½ teaspoon pepper
¼ teaspoon allspice
3 tablespoons lemon juice
3 egg yolks, lightly beaten
⅓ cup sliced black olives
¼ cup fresh parsley leaves

Brown lamb on all sides in hot oil in a large skillet. Place lamb, onion, lemon, bay leaf, and seasonings in slow cooker. Cover and cook on low 8 to 10 hours.

Place 1½ cups of the accumulated stock in a saucepan. Add lemon juice.

Spoon about ¼ cup warm stock into egg yolks, then stir diluted yolks back into stock. Heat gently, stirring constantly, until mixture thickens; do not boil.

Slice lamb, cover with thickened stock, and garnish with olives and parsley.

arabian lamb

Yield: 6 servings

2 pounds lamb, cut into 1-inch cubes
2 tablespoons vegetable oil
1½ cups water
1 stick cinnamon
1 onion, finely chopped
3 tablespoons raisins
4 ounces dried apricots
1 teaspoon salt

Brown lamb in hot oil in a large skillet. Place in slow cooker.

Add some of the water to the skillet and stir to pick up the browned bits. Add to the meat along with remaining water and all other ingredients. Cover and cook on low about 8 hours.

Pour accumulated gravy into a saucepan and boil until thickened and reduced by about half. Return to meat and fruit. Serve over freshly cooked rice.

lamb ragout with eggplant

Yield: 4 to 6 servings

1½ pounds lean lamb, cut into 1-inch
    cubes
¼ cup olive oil
3 onions, chopped
2 cloves garlic, minced
6 black peppercorns
1 8-ounce can tomato sauce

½ cup dry red wine
1½ teaspoons salt
4 tomatoes, peeled and cubed
1 medium eggplant, peeled,
    cut into ½-inch slices,
    and quartered
Chopped fresh parsley leaves

Brown lamb in hot olive oil in large skillet. Place in slow cooker with onions, garlic, peppercorns, tomato sauce, wine, and salt. Cover and cook on low about 8 hours.

Turn heat to high and add tomatoes and eggplant. Continue cooking until eggplant is tender, about 15 minutes. Serve at once garnished with parsley.

curried lamb ragout

Yield: 6 servings

1½ pounds lean lamb, cut into 1-inch cubes
2 tablespoons vegetable oil
1½ cups water
Grated rind of half a lemon
1 tart apple, peeled, cored, and cut into ½-inch cubes
1 large onion, sliced
½ teaspoon sage
1 teaspoon salt
2 tomatoes, peeled and cut into wedges
1 green pepper, cubed
1 4-ounce can mushrooms, drained
3 tablespoons all-purpose flour in 3 tablespoons cold water, mixed to a smooth
    paste
1 tablespoon curry powder
¼ cup sour cream

Brown lamb in oil in a large skillet. Add some of the water and stir to pick up the browned bits. Pour all into the slow cooker. Add remaining water, grated lemon rind, apple, onion, sage, and salt. Cover and cook on low about 8 hours.

Add tomatoes, green pepper, and mushrooms the last 10 minutes of cooking.

Pour juice into a saucepan, skim away excess fat, and add flour–water mixture and curry powder. Bring to a boil, stirring constantly until thickened. Stir in the sour cream. Return the mixture to the stew. Serve at once with boiled rice.

herbed lamb with squash

Yield: 6 to 8 servings

¾ pound Italian sausage, cut into 1-inch slices
1½ pounds lean lamb, cut into 1-inch cubes
1 cup dry red wine
1 8-ounce can tomato sauce
1 bay leaf
1 teaspoon each thyme, basil, paprika,
    black pepper, ginger, and oregano
1½ teaspoons salt
1 onion, chopped
1 small butternut squash, cut into 1-inch
    cubes
2 zucchini squash, cut into ½-inch slices
½ cup sliced mushrooms, browned in butter
Fresh mint leaves

Brown sausage pieces in large skillet. Place in slow cooker.
Brown lamb in accumulated fat. Place in slow cooker.
Drain fat from skillet and add wine. Stir to pick up browned bits, then pour into slow cooker along with all remaining ingredients except the mushrooms and mint leaves. Cover and cook on low about 8 hours.
Just before serving, add mushrooms. Garnish with fresh mint leaves.

lamb and pork with cabbage

Yield: 4 servings

½ pound lean lamb, cubed
½ pound lean pork, cubed
2 tablespoons vegetable oil
1 cup water
1 small head cabbage, coarsely shredded
4 potatoes, cubed
3 large onions, sliced
1 bay leaf
4 whole cloves
1½ teaspoons salt
Chopped fresh parsley leaves

Brown lamb and pork in hot oil in a large skillet. Place in the slow cooker.
Add a small amount of water to the skillet; stir to pick up the browned bits and add to the meat with remaining water and all of the other ingredients except parsley. Cover and cook on low about 8 hours. Garnish with chopped parsley.

baked ham

Yield: 6 to 8 servings

1 3-pound fully cooked ham
Whole cloves (optional)

Place ham in slow cooker. Ham may be scored diagonally and studded with whole cloves, if desired. Cover and cook on high for 3 to 4 hours. Serve with fresh or canned pineapple rings.

pork with apples

Yield: 6 servings

2½ pounds lean pork, cut into 1-inch cubes
2 tablespoons vegetable oil
1 tablespoon sugar
1½ teaspoons salt
2 teaspoons paprika
1½ cups apple cider
4 tart apples, peeled, cored, and cut into 1-inch cubes
¼ cup all-purpose flour in ¼ cup cold water, mixed to a paste
2 scallions, thinly sliced
Freshly ground black pepper

Brown pork in hot oil in a large skillet. Drain away accumulated fat. Place meat in slow cooker with sugar, salt, and paprika.

Add some of the cider to the skillet and stir to pick up the browned bits. Add to slow cooker. Cover and cook on low about 8 hours.

Add apples the last 3 hours of cooking.

Pour off juice and thicken in a saucepan with flour–water paste. Return to stew. Garnish with scallions and black pepper.

pork chops with raisins and oranges

Yield: 6 servings

6 lean pork chops, about 1 inch
    thick, well-trimmed
Flour, salt, and pepper
2 tablespoons vegetable oil

2 oranges, sections removed
    from membranes
¼ cup raisins

sauce

1 cup water
2 tablespoons cornstarch in
    2 tablespoons cold water,
    mixed until smooth

2 tablespoons lemon juice
2 tablespoons sugar
¼ teaspoon allspice

Dredge pork chops with flour that has been seasoned with salt and pepper. Brown in hot oil on both sides in a large skillet. Place in slow cooker with orange sections and raisins.

Combine sauce ingredients in a saucepan. Stir and heat until sauce boils and is thickened. Pour over pork and fruit in slow cooker. Cover and cook on low 5 to 6 hours. Spoon fruit and accumulated cooking liquid over chops when served.

veal stew

Beef may be substituted successfully for veal in this recipe.

Yield: 6 to 8 servings

4 slices bacon, cubed
2 pounds veal, cut into
    1-inch cubes
2¼ cups water
2 onions, coarsely chopped
2 cloves garlic, minced
6 carrots, sliced
1 cup converted rice (you must
    use *converted* rice)

1½ teaspoons salt
4 tomatoes, peeled and quartered
2 green peppers, cut into strips
Dash Tabasco sauce
2 tablespoons fresh parsley
    leaves, chopped

Cook bacon in a large skillet until transparent. Add veal and brown well. Place in slow cooker.

Add some of the water to the skillet and stir to pick up the browned bits. Add to veal along with remaining water, onions, garlic, carrots, rice, and salt. Cover and cook on low about 8 hours.

Add tomatoes, green peppers, and Tabasco sauce the last 10 minutes of cooking. Serve sprinkled with chopped parsley.

Picture on next page: veal stew

emperor's veal stew

Yield: 4 to 6 servings

    1½ pounds lean veal, cut into 1-inch cubes
    2 tablespoons bacon fat or vegetable oil
    Salt and pepper to taste
    2 medium onions, finely chopped
    ½ lemon, sliced
    1 cup hot water
    2 tablespoons flour in 2 tablespoons cold water, mixed to a smooth paste
    1½ cups sour cream
    1 tablespoon capers
    2 tablespoons lemon juice
    ½ teaspoon sugar

Brown meat in hot fat in a large skillet. Season to taste with salt and pepper. Add onions, lemon slices, and water and pour into slow cooker. Cover and cook on low about 8 hours.

Pour accumulated juices into a saucepan, add flour–water mixture, and bring to a boil, stirring constantly until thickened. Add sour cream, capers, lemon juice, and sugar. Heat briefly and recombine with meat. Serve at once.

emperor's veal stew

veal goulash

Yield: 6 servings

   1½ pounds veal or lean beef, cut into 1-inch cubes
   2 tablespoons vegetable oil
   3 onions, sliced
   1 6-ounce can tomato paste
   1½ tablespoons paprika
   1 teaspoon salt
   3 green peppers, cut into strips
   1 red pepper, cut into strips (allow a green pepper to ripen in your garden)
   1 cup yogurt

Brown veal in hot oil in a large skillet. Add a small amount of water to pick up the browned bits and pour all into the slow cooker. Add onions, tomato paste, paprika, and salt. Cover and cook on low about 8 hours.

Add peppers about 5 minutes before the end of cooking. Adjust seasoning.

Just before serving, partially fold in yogurt. Serve at once.

hungarian veal goulash

Yield: 4 servings

   1 pound lean veal, cut into 1-inch cubes
   2 tablespoons bacon fat
   2 medium onions, chopped
   ½ cup tomato paste
   1 teaspoon salt
   1 tablespoon paprika
   2 green peppers, cut into ¼-inch strips
   Dash Tabasco sauce

Brown veal in hot bacon fat in a large skillet. Place in slow cooker with onions and tomato paste. Sprinkle with salt and paprika. Cover and cook on low about 8 hours.

Add green peppers and Tabasco sauce 10 minutes before serving.

veal goulash

hot dogs and rolls

Yield: As needed

Hot dogs
Hot-dog rolls

Place hot dogs in slow cooker. Cover and cook on high 45 to 60 minutes. Add rolls the last 10 minutes of cooking. Serve at once.

hungarian
veal
goulash

chicken and lentil stew

Yield: 4 servings

½ pound dried lentils
2 carrots, diced
2 leeks or 3 scallions, sliced
1 teaspoon salt
½ teaspoon sage
¼ teaspoon pepper

1 slice lemon
1 2- to 3-pound frying chicken, cut up
2 to 3 tablespoons bacon fat or vegetable oil
2 cups water
¼ cup sour cream

Place the lentils, carrots, leeks, seasonings, and lemon slice in slow cooker.

Brown chicken in bacon fat or oil in a large skillet. Drain away excess fat. Place chicken in slow cooker on top of vegetables.

Add the water to the skillet and stir to loosen the browned bits. Pour into slow cooker. Cover and cook on low about 8 hours. Stir in sour cream and serve at once.

chicken and lentil stew

chicken stew with rice

Yield: 4 servings

2 stalks celery, cut into ¼-inch slices
4 carrots, cut into ¼-inch slices
¾ cup converted rice
1 2- to 3-pound frying chicken
2 cups water
1½ teaspoons salt
1 cup frozen, defrosted peas
Fresh parsley leaves

Place celery, carrots, and rice in the bottom of the slow cooker. Add chicken, water, and salt. Cover and cook on low about 8 hours.

Add peas the last 10 minutes of cooking.

Remove skin and bones from the chicken, cube the meat, and return it to the vegetables and rice. Ladle stew into bowls and garnish with fresh parsley leaves.

lentil–chicken stew

Yield: 6 servings

1 2- to 3-pound frying chicken, cut up
2 tablespoons vegetable oil or bacon fat
5 cups water
1 pound dried lentils
2 medium onions, chopped
Few sprigs winter savory or parsley
1½ teaspoons salt
2 teaspoons sugar
1 teaspoon thyme
Chopped parsley for garnish

Brown chicken in hot oil in a large skillet. Place in slow cooker.

Pour some of the water into the skillet and stir to pick up the browned bits. Add to the meat along with remaining water and all other ingredients. Cover and cook on low 6 to 8 hours.

Remove chicken, cube meat, and return to stew. Garnish with chopped fresh parsley leaves before serving.

lentil–chicken stew

barbecued chicken

Yield: 4 servings

1 2- to 3-pound frying chicken, cut up
½ cup tomato paste
¼ cup vinegar
1 tablespoon brown sugar
1 teaspoon salt

Place chicken in the slow cooker. Combine remaining ingredients and spoon over chicken. Cover and cook on low about 8 hours. Serve chicken with the cooking sauce.

57

chicken tarragon

The gravy is luscious and fragrant.

Yield: 4 servings

    1 3- to 4-pound frying chicken
    2 tablespoons soft butter or margarine
    1 teaspoon garlic salt
    1 teaspoon tarragon
    1 tablespoon dried parsley
    1/8 teaspoon freshly ground black pepper
    3 tablespoons vinegar

gravy

    2 tablespoons cornstarch in 2 tablespoons cold water, stirred until smooth
    1 cup accumulated cooking liquid

Rub chicken with butter; place in the slow cooker. Combine seasonings and herbs and sprinkle evenly over chicken. Add vinegar. Cover and cook on low about 8 hours. Do not remove lid during this time. Remove chicken to a hot platter.

Prepare the gravy by combining the cornstarch mixture and 1 cup of accumulated liquid in a saucepan. Heat and stir until mixture boils and is thickened. Serve over hot chicken.

oriental chicken

Yield: 4 servings

    1 2- to 3-pound frying chicken, cut up
    1/3 cup soy sauce
    2 tablespoons dry sherry
    2 tablespoons brown sugar
    1 teaspoon ginger or 2 slices fresh gingerroot
    1 clove garlic, minced
    2 tablespoons cornstarch in 2 tablespoons cold water, stirred until smooth
    1/4 cup slivered almonds

Place chicken in the slow cooker.

Combine soy sauce, sherry, brown sugar, ginger, and garlic. Pour over chicken. Cover and cook on low about 8 hours.

Pour cooking liquids into a measuring cup. Prepare gravy by combining 1 cup of the accumulated cooking liquid with the cornstarch mixture in a saucepan. Bring to a boil, stirring constantly until thickened. Serve over chicken. Garnish with slivered almonds.

58

marie's easy chicken and mushrooms

Yield: 4 servings

    1 2- to 3-pound frying chicken, cut up
    2 tablespoons vegetable oil
    1 10¾-ounce can cream of mushroom soup

Brown chicken in hot oil in a large skillet. Place in slow cooker. Add mushroom soup. Cover and cook on low about 8 hours. Serve chicken with accumulated gravy.

mandarin chicken with almonds

Yield: 4 servings

chicken

    1 teaspoon salt
    2 teaspoons paprika
    3-pound frying chicken, cut up
    3 tablespoons vegetable oil
    1 clove garlic
    2 tablespoons raisins
    ½ cup dry red wine

gravy

    1 cup accumulated cooking liquid
    2 tablespoons cornstarch in 2 tablespoons cold water, mixed to a smooth paste
    2 tablespoons soy sauce
    ½ teaspoon ground ginger
    1 11-ounce can mandarin oranges, drained
    ½ cup heavy cream or sour cream
    2 to 4 tablespoons sliced almonds

Combine salt and paprika and rub chicken pieces with the mixture. Brown chicken on all sides in hot oil in a heavy skillet, about 10 minutes. Place in the slow cooker with garlic and raisins.

Add the red wine to the skillet and stir to pick up the browned bits. Add to the chicken. Cover and cook on low about 8 hours.

Pour off accumulated cooking juices, reserving 1 cup. Place this in a saucepan with the cornstarch mixture, soy sauce, and ginger. Bring to a boil, stirring constantly until thickened. Add mandarin oranges. Blend in cream. Pour at once over chicken arranged on a hot platter. Garnish with almonds. Serve at once with rice.

Picture on next pages: mandarin chicken with almonds

chicken in orange sauce with cashews

Yield: 4 servings

  1 2- to 3-pound frying chicken, cut up
  ⅓ cup frozen orange-juice concentrate
  1 small onion, sliced thin
  1 teaspoon salt
  10 black peppercorns
  3 tablespoons all-purpose flour in 3 tablespoons cold water, mixed to a smooth
      paste
  ¼ cup cashew nuts, chopped

Place chicken in the slow cooker. Combine orange juice, onion, salt, and peppercorns. Pour over chicken. Cover and cook on low about 8 hours.

Remove chicken and pour juices into a saucepan. Add flour–water mixture. Heat and stir until mixture boils and is thickened. Serve over chicken. Garnish with cashew nuts.

pasta and sauces

manicotti

So good! Make it this way and you won't have to heat the oven.

Yield: 4 servings

    8 to 10 manicotti macaronis

filling

    1 pound ricotta cheese
    8 ounces mozzarella cheese, cut into ½-inch cubes
    ¼ cup grated Parmesan cheese
    1 egg
    ¼ teaspoon salt or garlic salt
    ½ teaspoon oregano
    1 tablespoon fresh parsley leaves, minced

sauce

    1 6-ounce can tomato paste
    1 cup water
    2 teaspoons oregano
    ½ teaspoon garlic salt
    1 tablespoon olive oil

Cook manicotti macaronis according to package directions; drain well.

Combine ingredients for the filling. Place about 3 tablespoons of this mixture inside each cooked manicotti. Place filled manicotti in slow cooker.

Combine ingredients for the sauce and pour over manicotti. Top with additional Parmesan cheese. Cover and cook on high 1¼ hours. Serve at once with Italian bread, tossed salad, and a dry red wine.

lasagna

This luscious oven dish can be prepared in your slow cooker. Serve with a tossed salad, hearty red wine, and toasted garlic bread.

Yield: 4 or 5 servings

    8 lasagna noodles, cooked according to package directions
    8 ounces ricotta cheese
    1 tablespoon dried parsley leaves
    ¼ cup grated Parmesan cheese
    8 ounces mozzarella cheese, thickly sliced

sauce

    ½ pound ground beef, browned in a skillet (optional, beef may be omitted)
    1 6-ounce can tomato paste
    2 ounces pepperoni, sliced
    ¾ cup water
    2 teaspoons oregano
    ¾ teaspoon garlic salt
    ¼ teaspoon freshly ground black pepper
    Parmesan cheese for topping (about 2 tablespoons)

Place half of the noodles in the bottom of the slow cooker. Spread with half the ricotta cheese, parsley, Parmesan cheese, mozzarella cheese, and sauce made by stirring together the sauce ingredients. Repeat. Top with additional Parmesan cheese. Cook on high 1 hour. Turn to low to keep warm if necessary. Serve hot.

ziti al forno

Yield: 6 to 8 servings

    1 pound ziti (extra-large macaroni), cooked according to package directions
    1 cup ricotta cheese
    1 16-ounce jar of your favorite prepared spaghetti sauce
    8 ounces mozzarella cheese, cut into ½-inch cubes
    Salt and pepper to taste
    ½ cup grated Parmesan cheese

Drain ziti well. Place in slow cooker. Gently combine with ricotta cheese and spaghetti sauce. Add mozzarella cheese, salt, and pepper. Toss lightly. Top with Parmesan cheese. Cover and cook on low about 1 hour, until heated through and mozzarella cheese is completely melted.

beef enchiladas

Yield: 4 servings

    8 to 10 corn tortillas

filling

1 pound extra-lean ground beef
    (sausage meat may be substituted
    for half of the beef)
¼ 8-ounce can tomato sauce
¼ 10-ounce can *mild*
    enchilada sauce
1 teaspoon salt

1 medium onion, chopped
½ cup raisins
3 tablespoons chopped, roasted,
    and peeled green chilies
    (available canned)
4 ounces cheddar cheese, shredded

sauce

¾ 8-ounce can tomato sauce
¾ 10-ounce can *mild*
    enchilada sauce

2 ounces cheddar cheese,
    shredded

Brown the beef in a skillet and drain well. Add the tomato and enchilada sauces and salt. Simmer 3 to 4 minutes, until thickened.

Place some of the meat mixture down the center of each tortilla. Sprinkle with chopped onions, raisins, chilies, and cheese. Roll and place, flap-side-down, in slow cooker.

Combine the remaining sauces and pour over the rolled tortillas. Top with cheese. Cover and cook on low about 1 to 1½ hours or until heated through. Serve at once with a cool beverage and a tossed salad.

chicken enchiladas

Yield: 3 or 4 servings

    8 corn tortillas

filling

2 cups coarsely chopped
    cooked chicken
¼ cup black olives, sliced

4 ounces mozzarella cheese, diced
½ cup sour cream
½ teaspoon salt

sauce

1 10-ounce can *mild*
    enchilada sauce
1 8-ounce can tomato sauce

Salt to taste
2 ounces mozzarella cheese,
    shredded

Combine filling ingredients and place some of the filling down the center of each tortilla. Roll, and place flap-side-down in the slow cooker.

Combine tomato and enchilada sauces and salt. Pour over the tortillas. Top with cheese. Cover and cook on low 1 to 1½ hours, until heated through. Serve at once.

ricotta and frijole casserole with chili peppers

An absolutely delicious vegetarian dish! My family has requested I tell you its appearance leaves much to be desired but it resembles lasagna in flavor.

Yield: 4 to 6 servings

2 cups cooked brown rice*
2 cups cooked black beans*
½ teaspoon garlic salt
8 ounces ricotta cheese
1 tablespoon dried parsley leaves
8 ounces mozzarella cheese, sliced

About 3 tablespoons canned chopped roasted chili peppers (available in the Mexican food section of your supermarket)
¼ cup grated Parmesan cheese

Combine rice, beans, and garlic salt. Place ⅓ of this mixture in slow cooker. Top with half of the ricotta cheese, parsley, mozzarella slices, and chili peppers. Repeat, ending with a layer of the bean–rice mixture. Top with Parmesan cheese. Heat on high for 1 hour.

Keep casserole warm for a short time, if necessary on low. Serve hot with a tossed salad. Dish may be garnished with parsley leaves or chopped tomatoes.

* Note: 1 cup black beans, soaked overnight, combined with 1 cup uncooked brown rice may be cooked in 5 cups water on high 2 to 3 hours, until tender. Drain away excess water before using in this recipe.

italian spaghetti sauce

Yield: 4 or 5 servings

1 pound extra-lean ground beef, browned and drained
1 12-ounce can tomato paste
2½ cups water
1 tablespoon oregano
1 teaspoon thyme
¼ teaspoon black pepper
1 teaspoon salt
2 tablespoons fresh parsley leaves, chopped
2 cloves garlic
¼ teaspoon fennel seed
12 ounces spaghetti noodles, cooked according to package directions

Combine all ingredients except the spaghetti in the slow cooker. Cover and cook on low 3 to 4 hours. Longer cooking diminishes the flavor. Serve sauce hot over prepared spaghetti noodles.

fresh tomato pasta sauce

An excellent way to use an abundant supply of garden-ripened tomatoes.

Yield: About 1 quart sauce, to serve 4

2 scallions, minced
1 clove garlic, minced
2 tablespoons butter
2 tablespoons olive oil
6 large tomatoes, skinned and
    coarsely chopped   (about 4 cups)

2 teaspoons oregano
¼ teaspoon freshly ground pepper
Salt to taste
Fresh parsley for garnish

Sauté scallions and garlic in a mixture of butter and olive oil in a small skillet until soft, about 3 minutes. Place in slow cooker along with all remaining ingredients. Cover and cook on low about 3 hours or until heated through. Serve at once over hot pasta. Garnish with parsley if you wish.

bolognese sauce

A traditional Italian spaghetti sauce to serve over your favorite pasta.

Yield: About 1 quart sauce, enough to serve 4

3 slices bacon
½ pound chicken livers
2 onions, chopped
1 carrot, chopped
1 stalk celery, chopped
1 pound extra-lean ground beef or veal
1 6-ounce can tomato paste

1½ cups dry white wine
1½ cups beef stock or bouillon
1 teaspoon oregano
½ teaspoon nutmeg
½ teaspoon freshly ground
    black pepper
Salt to taste

Brown the bacon and remove it from skillet. Lightly brown the chicken livers in the bacon fat. Remove and chop them; chop cooked bacon. Place both in slow cooker.

Add onions, carrot, and celery to skillet. Cook about 3 minutes, until soft. Place in the slow cooker.

Brown beef in skillet; drain and place in slow cooker. Add remaining ingredients to slow cooker. Cover and cook on low about 3 to 4 hours to blend flavors. Serve sauce over hot, well-drained pasta. Garnish with grated Parmesan cheese. Delicious!

vegetable, rice, and wheat dishes

artichokes

Yield: 4 servings

  4 small artichokes
  Juice of ½ lemon
  2 cups boiling water
  1 teaspoon salt
  Melted butter

Wash each artichoke; trim off the base. Cut about a 1-inch slice off the top. Using scissors, cut about ¼-inch from the tip of each leaf. Separate leaves and scoop out the hairy white choke with a spoon. Finally, rub the artichokes with lemon juice and place in slow cooker. Add water and salt, cover, and cook on low about 5 hours.

Serve with small bowls of melted butter. Only the lower thick parts of the leaves and the artichoke hearts are edible.

boston baked beans

My family's very favorite bean recipe. We love these served with Boston Brown Bread (see Index).

Yield: 6 to 8 servings

  1 pound dried navy beans
  6 cups water
  4 ounces salt pork, cut into 1-inch cubes
  2 teaspoons dry mustard
  2 teaspoons salt
  ½ teaspoon freshly ground black pepper
  ¾ cup molasses

Soak beans in water in the slow cooker overnight. Do not drain. Cover and cook on high 2 to 3 hours, until tender. Drain, reserving liquid. Add remaining ingredients and sufficient reserved liquid (about ¾ cup) to barely cover beans. Cover and cook on low 10 to 12 hours. Serve hot.

preparation of artichokes for cooking:

Cut off base and about a 1-inch slice from the top.

Trim about ¼ inch from the tip of each leaf.

Scoop out the hairy choke.

Rub with lemon juice.

orange beans

These have the zesty flavor of orange marmalade.

Yield: 6 to 8 servings

    1 pound dried navy beans
    6 cups water
    1 onion, chopped
    ¼ cup molasses
    2 cloves garlic, minced
    1 orange, sliced very thin
    2 teaspoons salt
    1 8-ounce can tomato sauce

Soak beans in water overnight in the slow cooker. Do not drain. Cover and cook on high 2 to 3 hours, until tender. Drain, reserving liquid. Add remaining ingredients and sufficient reserved liquid to barely cover beans. Cover and cook on low 8 to 10 hours. Serve hot.

cassoulet

Yield: 8 servings

    1 pound dried navy beans
    6 cups water
    8 ounces chicken meat, cubed
    4 ounces pepperoni, sliced
    1 tablespoon bacon fat
    1 bay leaf
    3 cloves garlic
    1 onion, chopped
    1 carrot, thinly sliced
    1 8-ounce can tomato sauce
    ½ cup dry red wine
    1½ teaspoons salt
    1 scallion, cut into ½-inch slices
    2 tablespoons bread crumbs

Soak beans overnight in water in slow cooker. Do not drain. Cover and cook on high 2 to 3 hours, until tender. Drain; reserve liquid.

Brown chicken and pepperoni in hot bacon fat in a skillet; drain away excess fat. Add to beans along with the bay leaf, garlic, onion, carrot, tomato sauce, wine, and salt. Add sufficient reserved bean cooking liquid to barely cover beans. Cover and cook on low 10 to 12 hours. Stir in sliced scallion and bread crumbs just before serving.

Picture on opposite page: cassoulet

apple–nut beans with honey and butter

Especially good with beef or pork.

Yield: 6 to 8 servings

 1 pound dried navy beans
 6 cups water
 2 slices fresh gingerroot
 2 teaspoons salt
 4 apples, cored, peeled, and cut into ¾-inch cubes
 ½ cup honey
 ¼ cup butter or margarine
 ½ cup, or more, coarsely chopped walnuts

Soak beans overnight in water in slow cooker. Do not drain. Cover and cook on high 2 to 3 hours, until tender. Drain; reserve liquid. Add ginger, salt, apples, honey, and sufficient reserved liquid to barely cover beans. Cover and cook on low about 8 hours.
Remove and discard ginger slices. Stir in butter and nuts just before serving.

pork and beans in tomato sauce

These are much better than any canned, popular brand. Make these for your next picnic.

Yield: 6 to 8 servings

 1 pound dried kidney beans or pink beans
 6 cups water
 1 pound smoked ham hocks
 1 8-ounce can tomato sauce
 ⅓ cup molasses
 1 teaspoon dry mustard
 1 teaspoon Worcestershire sauce
 2 teaspoons salt

Soak beans overnight in water in the slow cooker. Do not drain. Cover and cook on high 2 to 3 hours, until tender. Drain; reserve liquid. Add remaining ingredients and enough reserved liquid to barely cover beans. Cover and cook 10 to 12 hours on low. Remove ham, chop meat, and return meat to beans. Serve hot.

barbecue beans with burgundy wine

These beans have a wonderful smoky flavor. They're good!

Yield: 6 to 8 servings

  1 pound dried kidney beans
  6 cups water
  1 pound smoked ham hocks
  2 teaspoons salt
  2 tablespoons sugar
  2 teaspoons chili powder
  2 teaspoons Worcestershire sauce
  1 cup dry Burgundy
  1 8-ounce can tomato sauce
  1 onion, chopped

Soak beans overnight in water in the slow cooker. Do not drain. Cover and cook on high 2 to 3 hours, until tender. Drain; reserve liquid. Add remaining ingredients and enough reserved liquid (about ¾ cup) to barely cover beans. Cover and cook 10 to 12 hours on low.

Remove ham, chop it, and return meat to beans. Serve hot.

italian bean and cheese casserole

A scrumptious vegetarian main dish!

Yield: 4 servings

  1 16-ounce can kidney beans (1½ cups cooked)
  2 large onions, chopped
  2 cloves garlic, finely minced
  5 teaspoons dried basil
  1 teaspoon oregano
  2 teaspoons salt
  2 carrots, coarsely grated
  1 large stalk celery, chopped
  2 tomatoes, chopped
  1 cup (4 ounces) grated cheddar cheese

Combine beans, onions, garlic, herbs, and salt in slow cooker. Cover and heat on high 1 hour.

Stir in carrots, celery, and tomatoes. Top with cheese. Heat on high 10 minutes longer. Serve hot with buttered rice or bulgur.

mexican chili beans

Real south-of-the border hearty flavor.

Yield: 6 to 8 servings

   1 pound dried kidney beans
   6 cups water
   1 pound smoked ham hocks
   2 teaspoons salt
   2 cloves garlic
   ¼ teaspoon cinnamon
   ⅛ teaspoon cloves
   1 tablespoon dry mustard
   1 tablespoon chili powder
   2 tablespoons vinegar
   1 8-ounce can tomato sauce
   ½ cup strong black coffee
   1 onion, chopped fine
   4 ounces cheddar cheese, shredded

Soak beans in water overnight in the slow cooker. Do not drain. Cover and cook on high 2 to 3 hours, until tender. Drain; reserve liquid. Add remaining ingredients except onion and cheese. Add enough reserved liquid to barely cover beans. Cover and cook 10 to 12 hours on low.

Remove ham, chop meat, and return to beans. Stir in onion last 10 minutes of cooking. Serve hot. Garnish each portion with a generous sprinkling of shredded cheese.

sour-cream limas

Try these with pork or ham.

Yield: 6 to 8 servings

   1 pound dried baby lima beans
   6 cups water
   2 teaspoons salt
   1 scant cup sour cream
   1 green onion, sliced thin
   1 teaspoon basil
   ¼ cup fresh parsley leaves, chopped
   Freshly ground black pepper to taste

Soak beans overnight in water in the slow cooker. Do not drain. Add salt, cover, and cook 2 to 3 hours on high until tender. Drain.

Gently stir in remaining ingredients. Cook on low 1 hour. Serve while hot.

coffee beans

This dish really looks like coffee beans and has a mild red wine–coffee flavor.

Yield: 6 to 8 servings

> 1 pound black beans
> 6 cups water
> 2 tablespoons instant coffee
> ½ cup dry red wine
> ½ cup brown sugar
> 2 teaspoons salt
> 1 onion, chopped
> Parsley for garnish

Soak beans in water in slow cooker overnight. Do not drain. Cover and cook on high about 3 hours, until tender. Drain, reserving liquid.

Add remaining ingredients and sufficient reserved liquid to barely cover the beans. Cover and cook on low 6 to 8 hours. Serve hot garnished with parsley.

mexican beans

Yield: 6 to 8 servings

> ½ pound dried black beans
> 3 cups water
> 2 ounces salt pork
> 1 onion, peeled and left whole
> 1 teaspoon salt
> 1 10-ounce package frozen corn, defrosted
> Dash Tabasco sauce
> Sprig fresh mint leaves

Soak beans in water overnight in slow cooker. Do not drain. Add salt pork, cover, and cook on high 2 to 3 hours, until beans are tender.

Add remaining ingredients, cover, and continue heating on high until corn is heated through, 5 to 10 minutes. Serve hot. Garnish with mint leaves.

mexican beans

romanian bean pot

romanian bean pot

Yield: 6 to 8 servings

> ¼ pound dried pinto beans
> ¼ pound dried great northern or navy beans
> 3 cups water
> 4 slices bacon, cubed
> 1 large onion
> 1 clove garlic
> ½ teaspoon thyme
> 1 teaspoon salt
> ½ pound green beans, cut into 1-inch pieces
> ½ pound wax beans, cut into 1-inch pieces
> 2 teaspoons lemon juice

Place dried beans in slow cooker. Add water and soak overnight. Do not drain. Add bacon, onion, garlic, thyme, and salt. Cover and cook on high 2 to 3 hours, until beans are tender.

Add green beans and wax beans. Cover and cook on low about 20 minutes, until fresh beans are tender. Add lemon juice just before serving.

pizza beans

One of the best-liked recipes prepared by my students. You'll have many requests for it.

Yield: 4 servings

> 1 15-ounce can soy beans, undrained
> 1 cup canned tomatoes, drained
> 1 small onion, finely chopped
> ⅓ green pepper, chopped
> 1 clove garlic, minced
> 1 teaspoon salt
> ½ teaspoon oregano
> ¼ teaspoon rosemary
> 8 ounces mozzarella cheese, cut into ½-inch cubes
> 2 slices salami, cut into ¼-inch strips
> 3 tablespoons Parmesan cheese

Combine vegetables, spices, herbs, and mozzarella cheese in the slow cooker. Top with salami strips and sprinkle with Parmesan cheese. Cover and heat on high for 1 hour. Serve with tossed greens and garlic bread.

german gold and silver bean stew

Yield: 6 to 8 servings

1 pound dried great northern beans
6 cups water
1 pound lean beef, cut into ¾-inch cubes
2 tablespoons vegetable oil
4 carrots, cut into ½-inch cubes
2 teaspoons salt
1 10-ounce package frozen peas, defrosted

Soak beans in water in slow cooker overnight; do not drain. Cover and cook on high about 3 hours, until tender.

Brown beef in hot oil in a large skillet. Add to beans along with carrots and salt.

Add some of the bean cooking liquid to the skillet and stir to pick up the browned bits; pour into slow cooker. Cover and cook on low 8 to 10 hours. Add peas the last 10 minutes of cooking.

Ladle into bowls and serve with dark German rye bread.

german gold and silver bean stew

chick peas and ham

Yield: 6 to 8 servings

  1 pound dried chick peas
  6 cups water
  ½ pound lean ham, cut into
      ½-inch cubes
  2 teaspoons marjoram
  1 bay leaf
  2 onions, chopped
  2 carrots, cut into ½-inch cubes
  2 potatoes, cut into ½-inch cubes
  1 leek or 2 scallions, sliced
  2 teaspoons salt
  Chopped fresh parsley for garnish

Soak peas in water in the slow cooker overnight. Do not drain. Cover and cook on high 2 to 3 hours, until tender. Drain, reserving liquid.

Add all remaining ingredients, except parsley. Add enough reserved liquid barely to cover beans. Cover and cook on low about 8 hours. Serve in hot bowls garnished with parsley.

chick peas and ham

pineapple and beans

Very easy to prepare.

Yield: 6 to 8 servings

> 2 16-ounce cans baked beans
> 1 1-pound 13-ounce can pineapple chunks, drained
> 1 onion, finely chopped
> ⅓ cup molasses or dark corn syrup
> 1 teaspoon ground ginger or 3 slices fresh gingerroot

Combine all ingredients in slow cooker. Cover and cook on low 4 to 6 hours. Discard ginger slices before serving.

eggplant parmesan

Yield: 4 to 6 servings

> 2 eggs
> 1 teaspoon salt
> 1 large eggplant, pared and cut into
>   ⅓-inch slices
> Olive oil or vegetable oil
>
> 2 8-ounce cans tomato sauce
> 2 teaspoons oregano
> Garlic salt to taste
> ½ cup grated Parmesan cheese
> ½ pound sliced mozzarella cheese

Combine eggs and 1 teaspoon salt. Dip eggplant slices in this mixture and sauté in hot oil until golden brown on both sides.

Combine tomato sauce, oregano, and garlic salt.

Place half the eggplant slices in the bottom of the slow cooker. Top with half the Parmesan cheese and half the mozzarella cheese. Cover with half the tomato-sauce mixture. Repeat. Cover; cook on low about 1 hour, until heated through.

eggplant mozzarella

Yield: 6 servings

> 2 7-ounce packages frozen
>   fried eggplant slices
> 8 ounces mozzarella cheese, sliced
> 2 tablespoons fresh parsley leaves,
>   chopped
>
> ½ teaspoon garlic salt
> Freshly ground black pepper
> 1 8-ounce can tomato sauce
> 2 tablespoons grated Parmesan cheese

Place half of eggplant slices in slow cooker. Top with half of the mozzarella cheese, parsley, garlic salt, pepper, and tomato sauce. Repeat. Sprinkle Parmesan cheese over the top. Cover and cook on high 1 hour, until heated through.

danish red cabbage

Yield: 6 servings

    1 small head red cabbage, shredded
    1 apple, peeled, cored, and cubed
    4 slices bacon, cubed
    1 onion, sliced
    1 tablespoon vinegar
    1 tablespoon lemon juice
    2 tablespoons red wine
    2 tablespoons sugar
    Pinch allspice
    Salt and pepper to taste

Place all ingredients in slow cooker. Cover and cook on low about 3 hours or until tender.

danish red cabbage

rotkuhl

Another version of Danish red cabbage. This one contains more fruit and is especially good.

Yield: 6 to 8 servings

> 1½ pounds red cabbage, shredded
> 1 apple, peeled, cored, and coarsely chopped
> ¼ cup raisins
> 2 tablespoons butter or margarine
> 1 tablespoon vinegar
> ¼ cup water
> ¼ cup raspberry (or other red) jelly
> Salt and pepper to taste

Place all ingredients in slow cooker. Cover and cook on low about 3 hours or until tender.

This may be made a day ahead, refrigerated, and reheated just before serving.

baked potatoes

Yield: Varies with number used

Baking potatoes

Stack clean baking potatoes in slow cooker. Cover and cook on low about 8 to 10 hours, until tender.

sauerkraut and knockwurst

Yield: 4 servings

> 1 16-ounce can sauerkraut, drained, and rinsed several times in cold water
> 2 apples, cored, peeled, and cut into ½-inch cubes
> 1 onion, sliced
> ¼ teaspoon caraway seeds
> ¼ cup water
> 4 knockwursts

Combine sauerkraut, apples, onion, and seasonings in slow cooker. Add knockwurst; cook on low 4 to 5 hours.

acorn squash stuffed with sausage and apples

The combination of spicy sausage and apples in the stuffing is quite good with the mild squash. This dish is best for four persons, as more halved stuffed squashes will not fit inside a 3½-quart cooker.

Yield: 4 servings

> 1 pound sausage meat
> 1 small onion, chopped
> 2 apples, cored and chopped
> ½ teaspoon oregano
> Salt to taste
> 2 acorn squashes, halved, seeds removed
> ¼ cup water

Brown sausage meat well and break into small pieces. Drain well. Combine meat with onion, apples, oregano, and salt. Generously fill each squash half with the mixture and arrange filled halves in the slow cooker in staggered layers. Pour about ¼ cup water into the bottom of the cooker. Cover and cook on low for 6 to 8 hours, until squash is tender. Serve at once with hot buttered rice.

baked butternut squash and fruit

A fragrant dish with spicy overtones.

Yield: 6 servings

> 1 2-pound butternut squash, quartered, seeded, peeled, and cut into ¼-inch slices
> 3 apples, cored and cut into ¼-inch round slices
> ¼ cup raisins
> ½ lemon, cut into 4 round slices
> ½ cup brown sugar
> 1 teaspoon salt
> ½ teaspoon cinnamon
> 4 tablespoons butter or margarine

Combine squash, apples, and raisins in slow cooker. Arrange lemon slices on top. Sprinkle with sugar, salt, and cinnamon. Dot with butter. Cover and cook on low 4 to 6 hours. Serve hot in small bowls with the rich, zesty sauce.

zucchini-squash bake

Squash with an Italian flavor.

Yield: 4 to 6 servings

2 large zucchini squashes, unpeeled,
    cut into ½-inch slices
1 cup canned tomatoes, well-drained
1 tablespoon olive oil
1 small onion, chopped
1 clove garlic, minced

½ teaspoon salt
½ teaspoon basil
¼ teaspoon freshly ground
    black pepper
2 tablespoons grated
    Parmesan cheese

Combine all ingredients except cheese in the slow cooker. Cover and cook on low 4 to 5 hours. Sprinkle with cheese just before serving.

buttered converted rice

Perfect rice every time!

Yield: 4 to 6 servings

1 cup converted rice
2½ cups water
2 teaspoons salt
2 tablespoons butter

Combine all ingredients in the slow cooker and cook on low 6 to 8 hours or until all the water is absorbed.

Rice should be stirred several times during cooking to prevent top layer from drying and to assure even water absorption.

steamed short- or long-grain rice

Long- or short-grain rice must be cooked on high to soften the starch in the grain. Use this method for rice that is not the converted type.

Yield: 3 cups

1 cup rice
2 cups water
1 teaspoon salt

Combine all ingredients in slow cooker. Cover and cook on high, stirring occasionally to prevent surface grains from drying, for 1½ to 2 hours.

buttered cracked wheat (bulgur)

A nutty-flavored grain that makes a nice change from rice or a good substitute for corn or potatoes at dinner.

Yield: 4 to 6 servings

> **1 cup bulgur (toasted cracked wheat, available in natural food stores)**
> **2 cups water**
> **1 teaspoon salt**
> **2 tablespoons butter**

Combine all ingredients in slow cooker and cook on low 6 to 8 hours or until all the water is absorbed. Stir occasionally to prevent top layer from drying. Serve hot with additional butter.

bulgur pilaf

Yield: 6 servings

> **1 cup bulgur (toasted cracked wheat, available in natural food stores)**
> **2 cups beef or chicken broth**
> **1 tomato, chopped**
> **1 small onion, chopped**
> **¼ cup fresh parsley leaves, chopped**
> **½ teaspoon salt**
> **¼ teaspoon freshly ground black pepper**

Combine all ingredients in slow cooker. Cover and cook on low 6 to 8 hours, stirring occasionally.

house bean soup

A simple-to-make, filling soup served every day in the United States House of Representatives cafeteria. Try the Senate Bean Soup also.

Yield: 8 servings

>1 pound dried navy beans
>7 or 8 cups water
>1 pound smoked ham hocks
>Salt and freshly ground pepper to taste

Soak beans in water overnight in the slow cooker. Do not drain. Cover and cook on high about 3 hours, until tender.

Add ham and seasonings. Cover and cook on low 10 to 12 hours.

Remove ham, chop meat, and return it to soup. Add more water if you wish, and adjust seasonings. Serve hot for lunch.

senate bean soup

Your soup will have more meat in it, otherwise this is the hearty soup served every day in the United States Senate's cafeteria.

Yield: 8 servings

>1 pound dried navy beans
>7 or 8 cups water (approximately)
>1 pound smoked ham hocks
>2 onions, finely chopped
>4 stalks celery with leaves, finely chopped
>1 clove garlic, minced
>¼ cup fresh parsley leaves, finely chopped
>Salt and freshly ground black pepper to taste

Soak beans in the water overnight in the slow cooker. Do not drain. Cover and cook on high about 3 hours, until very tender.

Add remaining ingredients, except salt and pepper, cover, and cook on low 10 to 12 hours.

Remove ham, chop meat, and return it to soup. Season to taste with salt and pepper. More water may be added if soup seems too thick. Serve piping hot in large soup bowls—a meal in itself!

navy bean soup

Yield: 8 servings

1 pound dried navy beans
6 cups water
½ pound lean beef, cut into 1-inch cubes, and browned in bacon fat
1 medium onion, chopped
1 clove garlic
1 8-ounce can tomato sauce
2 tablespoons vinegar
½ teaspoon rosemary or caraway seeds
1 bay leaf
2 teaspoons salt
Chopped fresh chives

Soak beans in water in the slow cooker overnight. Do not drain. Cover and cook on high about 3 hours, until tender.

Add remaining ingredients, except chives. Cover and cook on low about 8 hours. Serve hot, garnished with chopped chives.

navy bean soup

bean soup with frankfurters

Yield: 6 to 8 servings

> 1 pound dried great northern or navy beans
> 7 or 8 cups water
> 1 carrot, diced
> 1 stalk celery with leaves, diced
> 1 large onion, chopped
> 2 teaspoons salt
> ¼ teaspoon pepper
> 2 or 3 frankfurters, sliced
> 2 tablespoons fresh parsley leaves, chopped

Soak beans overnight in water in the slow cooker. Do not drain. Cover and cook on high about 3 hours, until tender.

Add vegetables and seasonings. Cover and cook on low 10 to 12 hours.

Add frankfurters the last 30 minutes of cooking. Stir to mash some of the beans and thicken the soup. Serve hot, garnished with fresh parsley.

bean soup with frankfurters

westphalian blindhuhn

Yield: 6 servings

 ½ pound dried great northern beans
 3 to 4 cups water
 ⅓ pound slab bacon
 4 carrots, sliced
 2 potatoes, cubed
 2 tart apples, peeled, cored, and quartered
 2 pears, peeled, cored, and quartered
 1 teaspoon sugar
 Salt and pepper to taste
 1 cup green beans, cut into 1-inch pieces

Place beans in slow cooker. Add water and let soak overnight. Do not drain. Add bacon, cover, and cook on high 2 to 3 hours or until beans are tender.

Add carrots, potatoes, fruits, and seasonings. Cover and cook on low about 8 hours.

Add green beans the last 10 minutes of cooking. Remove bacon and cut it into slices. Serve soup in hot bowls with bacon arranged on top.

westphalian blindhuhn

french bean and potato soup

Yield: 6 servings

½ pound dried great northern or navy beans
6 cups water
½ cup dry red wine
12 ounces lean salt pork or smoked ham, cut into 1-inch cubes
3 potatoes, cubed
2 cloves garlic
1½ teaspoons salt
¼ teaspoon black pepper
1 10-ounce package frozen green beans, defrosted
3 tomatoes, peeled and cubed
Fresh parsley, chopped

Soak beans in water overnight in the slow cooker. Do not drain. Add wine, pork, potatoes, garlic, salt, and pepper. Cover and cook on high about 3 hours, until beans and potatoes are tender.

Add green beans and tomatoes and continue cooking on high 10 minutes longer. Serve at once garnished with fresh parsley.

chunky-style split-pea soup with ham

This soup is a meal by itself. You'll have many requests to serve this again.

Yield: 8 servings

1 pound dried split peas
6 cups hot water
1 pound smoked ham hocks
3 carrots, cut into ½-inch cubes
2 potatoes, cut into ½-inch cubes
1 onion, chopped

2 stalks celery, chopped
2 teaspoons salt
12 peppercorns
Parmesan cheese, grated,
    for garnish

Combine all ingredients except cheese in the slow cooker. Cover and cook on low 5 to 6 hours. Turn heat to high and cook an additional 1 to 1½ hours or until peas and vegetables are tender.

Remove ham; cube meat and return it to soup. Stir to mash some of the peas and thicken soup. Add additional water if you wish to thin the consistency. Garnish with grated Parmesan cheese when served.

Picture on opposite page: french bean and potato soup

hearty lentil soup

Good and substantial.

Yield: 8 servings

    1 pound dried lentils
    1 pound smoked ham hocks
    6 cups water
    4 stalks celery with leaves, chopped
    2 carrots, cut into ½-inch cubes
    1 large onion, chopped
    1 teaspoon salt
    ¼ teaspoon pepper

Combine all ingredients in the slow cooker. Cover and cook on low 6 to 8 hours. Stir to mash some of the lentils and thicken the soup.

Remove ham; cube meat and return it to soup. Additional water may be added if a thinner consistency is desired.

homestyle lentil soup

Yield: 8 servings

    1 pound dried lentils
    6 cups water
    2 medium onions, chopped
    4 carrots, sliced, cubed, or trimmed in the shape of round balls
    1 teaspoon thyme
    1 bay leaf
    1 teaspoon salt
    2 tablespoons sugar
    10 whole black peppercorns
    4 to 5 ounces heavily cured ham or Canadian bacon, cut into ½-inch cubes
    ½ cup dry red wine

Combine all ingredients, except for the wine, in the slow cooker. Cover and cook on low 6 to 8 hours.

Just before serving, stir in the red wine. Adjust seasonings, if necessary. Additional water may be added for a thinner consistency.

Picture on opposite page: homestyle lentil soup

french onion soup

Yield: 4 or 5 servings

3 cups thinly sliced onions
3 tablespoons oil
4 to 5 cups rich beef stock or Brown Beef Broth (see Index)
½ cup vermouth
4 or 5 thick slices dry French bread
3 ounces grated Swiss cheese
¼ cup grated Parmesan cheese

Place onions and oil in a large skillet. Cover and cook over low heat until soft, about 10 minutes. Uncover, turn up heat, and cook onions until they are a rich, mahogany brown, about 10 minutes or longer. Stir every 2 or 3 minutes and do not burn.

Place onions in the slow cooker with beef stock. Cover and cook on low 4 to 6 hours.

Add vermouth. Place soup in bowls. Top each with a slice of French bread; sprinkle with a mixture of Swiss and Parmesan cheeses.

Place under the broiler just until cheese melts. Serve at once.

julienne vegetable soup

Yield: 6 servings

2 medium onions, sliced
½ pound carrots, cut into julienne strips
2 celery stalks, cut into julienne strips
2 leeks, sliced
3 kohlrabi or turnips, cut into julienne strips
5 cups Brown Beef Broth (see Index) or bouillon
1½ teaspoons salt
1 teaspoon dried chervil
⅛ teaspoon pepper
Fresh parsley leaves

Combine all ingredients, except the chervil, pepper, and parsley, in the slow cooker. Cover and cook on low 4 to 5 hours or until vegetables are tender.

Add chervil and pepper 10 minutes before soup is done. Ladle into large bowls and garnish with parsley.

Picture on opposite page: julienne vegetable soup

spinach soup

Yield: 6 servings

1½ pounds lean beef with bones
6 cups water
1½ teaspoons salt
6 medium potatoes, cubed
3 onions, sliced

1½ pounds fresh spinach, washed and
    coarsely chopped
4 tomatoes, peeled and cut into wedges
Nutmeg and freshly ground black pepper

Combine beef, water, salt, potatoes, and onions in slow cooker. Cover and cook on low about 8 hours.

Add spinach and tomatoes the last 10 minutes of cooking

Remove meat from soup, cut it into 1-inch cubes, and return it to soup. Season with nutmeg and pepper. Add additional salt if desired.

brown beef broth or bouillon

Yield: 6 cups

2 pounds beef shanks (or 2
    pounds beef—about ⅓ should
    be bones)
2 tablespoons vegetable oil
6 cups water

4 whole black peppercorns
2 carrots, quartered
2 onions, quartered
1½ teaspoons salt

Brown meat on all sides in a large skillet. Place meat in the slow cooker.

Add some of the water to the skillet and stir to pick up the browned bits. Add to the meat along with remaining water, vegetables, and salt. Cover and cook on low about 10 hours.

Strain broth before using in soups or other recipes.

chicken broth or stock

Yield: 6 cups

2 pounds chicken with bones, cut up
6 cups water
1 small onion, chopped
1 large stalk celery with leaves, chopped
4 whole black peppercorns
1½ teaspoons salt

Combine all ingredients in slow cooker. Cover; cook on low about 10 hours.

Strain broth before using in other recipes.

This broth may be used whenever a recipe calls for white stock. It is good also for use in the gravy of Oriental stir-fry dishes.

Picture on opposite page: spinach soup

consommé

This is a clear soup usually made from two kinds of meat or meat and poultry.

Yield: 6 cups

1 pound lean beef,
    cut into 1-inch cubes
1 pound lean veal, cut into
    1-inch cubes (1 pound
    cut-up chicken with bones
    may be substituted)
6 cups water

1 carrot, chopped
1 stalk celery with leaves, chopped
1 onion, chopped
4 whole black peppercorns
2 whole cloves
1 teaspoon dried herbs (your favorite)
1½ teaspoons salt

Combine all ingredients in slow cooker. Cover and cook on low about 10 hours.

Clarify soup by pouring it through several layers of cheesecloth. Skim off fat. Serve very hot.

barley soup with beef and vegetables

Best you've ever made!

Yield: 6 to 8 servings

½ pound lean beef, cut into ½-inch cubes
1 tablespoon vegetable oil
6 cups water
4 carrots, cut into ½-inch cubes
2 stalks celery with leaves, cut into ½-inch cubes
4 green onions, cut into ¼-inch slices
¼ cup fresh parsley leaves, chopped
1 tomato, peeled and chopped
½ cup barley
1½ teaspoons salt
½ teaspoon whole peppercorns
½ teaspoon thyme

Brown meat in hot oil in a skillet. Add a little of the water to the skillet and stir to pick up browned bits.

Pour into slow cooker. Add remaining water and all other ingredients except the thyme. Cover and cook on low 4 to 6 hours, until vegetables and barley are tender. Add thyme just before serving.

russian borscht

russian sauerkraut soup

italian minestrone

italian minestrone

Yield: 6 servings

1 pound lean beef,
    cut into ½-inch cubes
5 cups water
2 medium onions, chopped
1 stalk celery, chopped
4 carrots, cut into small
    bite-size sticks
2 turnips, cubed
1 medium potato, cubed
1 clove garlic
1 teaspoon salt

½ small head cabbage,
    finely shredded
2 ounces macaroni, cooked
    according to package
    directions and drained
½ cup cooked rice (optional)
2 or 3 peeled tomatoes,
    cut into small wedges
Chopped fresh parsley
Grated Parmesan cheese

Combine beef, water, onions, celery, carrots, turnips, potato, garlic, and salt. Cover and cook on low about 8 hours.

Turn heat to high the last 20 minutes of cooking and add cabbage.

Add the cooked macaroni, rice, and tomatoes the last 10 minutes of cooking on high.

Ladle at once into bowls and serve with parsley and grated Parmesan cheese or Pesto Sauce (see Index).

Left to right:
 venetian minestrone
 swiss minestrone
 neopolitan minestrone

106

swiss minestrone

Yield: 6 to 8 servings

1½ pounds beef shanks
2 tablespoons vegetable oil
5 cups water
4 medium potatoes, diced
5 carrots, sliced
3 stalks celery, sliced
1 cup cubed pumpkin, if available
1 onion, chopped
2 scallions, sliced

½ pound cabbage, shredded
1 8-ounce can tomato sauce
1½ teaspoons salt
1 cup cooked rice
1 10-ounce package frozen green beans, defrosted
¼ teaspoon rosemary
¼ teaspoon sage
Chopped parsley

Brown beef shanks in hot oil in a large skillet. Place in slow cooker.

Add some of the water to the skillet and stir to pick up the browned bits. Add to the slow cooker along with the potatoes, carrots, celery, pumpkin, onion, scallions, cabbage, tomato sauce, and salt. Cover and cook on low about 8 hours.

Remove meat, cube, and return it to soup. Add cooked rice, beans, rosemary, and sage. Cover and continue cooking on high about 10 minutes. Serve soup hot, garnished with parsley.

venetian minestrone

Yield: 6 to 8 servings

1½ pounds beef shank
1 medium onion
5 whole cloves
1 clove garlic
6 cups water
1 bay leaf
½ teaspoon rosemary
5 whole black peppercorns
1½ teaspoons salt
3 slices bacon, cut into small pieces

1 onion, chopped
½ pound cabbage, shredded
4 tomatoes, peeled and chopped
1 teaspoon oregano
½ cup rice, cooked according to package directions
6 ounces calves liver, cooked and cubed
4 ounces grated Parmesan cheese
Chopped fresh parsley

Place shanks, whole onion studded with cloves, garlic, water, bay leaf, rosemary, peppercorns, and salt in slow cooker. Cover and cook on low 6 to 8 hours.

Strain and return broth to slow cooker. Cut meat into bite-size pieces and return to broth.

Brown bacon and onion in a skillet until bacon is crisp and onions are golden. Add to meat and broth. Add cabbage, tomatoes, oregano, and cooked rice. Cover and cook on high about 10 to 15 minutes.

Top soup with cubed liver, Parmesan cheese, and parsley. Serve piping hot.

pesto sauce for minestrone soups

Stir a little of this sauce into any vegetable or minestrone soup just before serving.

Yield: About 1 cup

> 1 cup fresh basil leaves or fresh parsley leaves
> ½ cup grated Parmesan cheese
> ¼ cup olive oil
> 1 clove garlic

Place all ingredients in a blender and blend at high speed until smooth. Use at once or cover and refrigerate no more than a week.

bunte finken
(german pork–vegetable soup)

Yield: 6 servings

> ½ pound dried navy beans
> 5 cups water
> 1 pound lean pork or ham, cut into 1-inch cubes
> 1½ teaspoons salt
> 4 carrots, cut into ½ × 1-inch strips
> 2 parsnips or small turnips, cubed
> 1 large onion, sliced
> 2 potatoes, cubed
> 1 cup frozen, defrosted green beans
> 2 tablespoons fresh parsley leaves, chopped

Soak navy beans in water in slow cooker overnight. Do not drain. Add pork or ham and salt. Cover and cook on high 1 to 2 hours, until beans are tender.

Add all remaining ingredients except green beans and parsley. Cover and cook on low 5 to 6 hours or until vegetables are tender.

Add green beans the last 10 minutes of cooking. Serve hot in large bowls; garnish with fresh parsley.

scottish lamb soup

Yield: 4 servings

**1 pound lean lamb, cut
    into 1-inch cubes
2 tablespoons vegetable oil
6 cups water
1½ teaspoons salt
2 carrots, sliced
3 parsnips, sliced
3 leeks, sliced
1 pound small potatoes, peeled
½ cup barley
1 tablespoon sugar
1 tablespoon dried mint leaves
Tarragon vinegar to taste
Fresh parsley leaves**

Brown lamb in a large skillet in hot oil. Place in slow cooker.

Add some of the water to the skillet and stir to pick up the browned bits. Add to meat with remaining water, salt, vegetables, barley, sugar, and mint leaves. Cover and cook on low about 6 hours. Season to taste with a little tarragon vinegar. Serve very hot garnished with parsley.

scottish lamb soup

lamb and vegetable soup

Yield: 5 to 6 servings

1 pound lean lamb, cut
    into bite-size cubes
2 tablespoons vegetable oil
5 cups water
2 tablespoons tomato paste
1 medium onion, chopped
2 stalks celery with leaves, sliced
4 carrots, sliced
2 potatoes, cut into ½-inch cubes
1 leek, sliced (optional)

½ small head cabbage, coarsely shredded
Salt and pepper to taste
1 10-ounce package frozen cauliflower,
    defrosted
1 cup frozen green beans, defrosted
1 cup fresh spinach leaves, torn into
    bite-size pieces
2 tablespoons fresh parsley leaves,
    chopped

Brown lamb in hot oil in a large skillet. Add a little of the water and stir to pick up the browned bits. Pour into the slow cooker along with remaining water, tomato paste, onion, celery, carrots, potatoes, leek, cabbage, salt, and pepper. Cover and cook on low about 8 hours.

Turn heat to high and add cauliflower and green beans. Cook 10 to 15 minutes longer. Just before serving, stir in spinach and parsley. Serve at once.

lamb and vegetable soup

shrimp soup

Yield: 4 or 5 servings

4 ounces cooked ham, cubed
2 slices bacon, cubed
4 cups hot water or beef broth
⅓ cup tomato paste
3 tablespoons catsup
½ cup converted rice
3 tomatoes, peeled and cubed

12 green olives, coarsely chopped
1 tablespoon capers
½ teaspoon oregano
¼ teaspoon coriander
10 ounces frozen or fresh cleaned
    and deveined shrimp
Salt and pepper to taste

Brown ham and bacon in a skillet. Place in slow cooker with water, tomato paste, catsup, rice, and tomatoes. Cover and cook on low about 3 hours or until rice is tender.

Turn heat to high. Add remaining ingredients and cook on high 5 to 10 minutes or just until shrimp has heated through. Serve at once.

fish chowder

The stock portion of this recipe can be used in your own fish-chowder recipes.

Yield: 4 to 6 servings

fish stock

1 large fish head
1 bay leaf
1 large onion, chopped
1 clove garlic
4 potatoes, cubed
1 teaspoon salt
¼ teaspoon pepper

soup ingredients

1½ pounds fish fillets,
    cut into bite-size pieces
2 tablespoons vegetable or olive oil
2 peeled tomatoes, cut into wedges
3 tablespoons chopped stuffed olives
1 to 2 tablespoons capers
1 tablespoon lemon juice
Fresh parsley leaves, chopped

Prepare stock by combining all stock ingredients in slow cooker. Cover and cook on low 5 or 6 hours or until potatoes are tender. Remove fish head and garlic.

Brown fish lightly in hot oil in a large skillet. Add to stock mixture along with tomatoes, olives, capers, and lemon juice. Cook on high about 10 minutes.

Ladle into bowls and garnish with fresh parsley. Serve with crackers or hard rolls.

Picture on next pages: bunte finken

fish chowder with white wine

Yield: 5 or 6 servings

2 slices bacon
2 medium onions, chopped
1 clove garlic
¼ cup tomato paste
2 cups beef broth
1 cup dry white wine
4 tomatoes, peeled and cubed

2 teaspoons paprika
Salt to taste
1 tablespoon lemon juice
1 to 1½ pounds fish fillets, cut into
bite-size pieces
Chopped fresh parsley leaves

Brown bacon in a large skillet. Remove, crumble, and place in slow cooker. Brown onions and garlic in the accumulated bacon fat. Pour into the slow cooker along with all remaining ingredients except the fish and parsley. Cover and cook on high for 1 hour.

Add fish and continue to cook on high 10 to 15 minutes or until fish is tender.

Serve at once or keep warm on low for about an hour. Overcooking will make fish tough. Garnish with chopped parsley.

hungarian apple soup

Yield: 4 servings

4 tart apples, peeled, cored, and diced
2 small onions, chopped
1 clove garlic, minced
2 green peppers, diced
1 red pepper, diced
1 cucumber, peeled and diced
2 cups beef stock
Salt to taste
2 teaspoons paprika
½ cup sour cream
2 tablespoons chopped fresh chives or thinly sliced scallions

Combine apples, onions, garlic, peppers, cucumber, and beef stock in slow cooker. Add salt to taste. Cover and cook on low 4 to 5 hours or until apples and vegetables are tender.

Add paprika and sour cream. Serve hot, garnished with chives or thinly sliced scallions.

Picture on opposite page: shrimp soup
Picture on next page: fish chowder

yugoslavian apple soup

Yield:4 servings

6 tart apples, cored, peeled, and sliced
2 cups water
1 cup dry white wine
2 tablespoons sugar
1 teaspoon cinnamon
Juice of half a lemon
3 tablespoons butter
Croutons for garnish

Combine apples, water, wine, sugar, cinnamon, and lemon juice in slow cooker. Cover and cook on low about 6 hours or until apples are very soft.

Add butter. Puree in a food mill. Serve hot, garnished with croutons.

Picture on next page:
top: yugoslavian apple soup
bottom: hungarian apple soup

117

breads

boston brown bread

This New England bread is made with three grains, molasses, and raisins. I have recommended a large amount of rye flour to keep the bread as compact as that found in cans at the supermarket. Serve this with Boston Baked Beans (see Index). *Note: You will need 3 empty 15- or 16-ounce vegetable cans for the small loaves.*

Yield: 1 5-cup loaf or 3 15-ounce can loaves

1 tablespoon vegetable oil
1 egg
½ cup molasses
1 cup buttermilk (or 1 cup milk plus ½ tablespoon vinegar)
½ cup raisins
1 cup rye flour
½ cup whole-wheat flour
⅓ cup cornmeal
1 teaspoon baking soda
1 teaspoon salt

Turn the slow cooker high. Butter a 5-cup mold or 3 15- or 16-ounce vegetable cans. Boil about 2 cups water and set aside.

Combine liquid ingredients and raisins.

Stir together the dry ingredients.

Stir the wet ingredients into the dry ingredients all at once just until blended. Do not overmix. Pour immediately into a prepared mold or cans (fill only ⅔ full). Cover mold or cans with aluminum foil and tie it on with string. Place in the slow cooker. Add boiling water to come halfway up the sides of the molds. Cook on high 2 to 3 hours.

Remove from slow cooker and cool 10 minutes. Invert mold or cans to remove bread. Cool completely on a wire rack. Serve with butter or cream cheese.

round light rye sandwich bread

Yield: 1 loaf

1 package active dry yeast
1 cup warm water (105–115°F)
1 tablespoon molasses
2 tablespoons vegetable oil
1 tablespoon caraway seeds
1½ cups all-purpose flour
1½ cups rye flour
1½ teaspoons salt

Dissolve yeast in warm water in a large bowl. Add molasses, oil, seeds, and all-purpose flour. Stir vigorously until smooth. Cover bowl and let stand in a warm place for ½ hour.

Stir in the rye flour and salt. Knead on a lightly floured surface until smooth, about 1 to 2 minutes.

Pat into a greased 48-ounce fruit-juice can, trimmed (see front of book) to barely fit under the lid of the covered slow cooker. Place can in slow cooker. Cover and cook on high for 2 hours. Do not remove lid even if the loaf rises and touches it. Loaf is done when a skewer inserted into loaf comes out clean.

Cool bread in can about ½ hour. Invert and shake to loosen. Cool on a wire rack. Serve warm.

swedish limpa round rye bread

This loaf has an orange–licorice flavor and complements ham and cheese slices well.

Yield: 1 loaf

In the preceeding recipe for Light Rye Bread, add to the dissolved yeast mixture:

1 teaspoon anise seeds
Grated rind of 1 orange
3 tablespoons of sugar in place of the molasses

Follow recipe directions as given.

120

round raisin whole-wheat bread

Serve during a meal—very moist and delicate.
Note: A 3-pound shortening can or 6- to 8-cup mold is needed.

Yield: 1 round loaf

1 cup buttermilk
1 egg
¼ cup molasses
2 tablespoons vegetable oil
2 tablespoons sugar
¾ cup raisins, cut up

¼ cup chopped nuts
1 cup whole-wheat flour
1 cup sifted all-purpose flour
1 teaspoon baking powder
1 teaspoon baking soda

Combine buttermilk, egg, molasses, oil, and sugar. Beat until well-blended. Add raisins and nuts.

Stir together the flours, baking powder, and baking soda. Add the buttermilk mixture and stir only until the dry ingredients are moistened.

Pour into a greased 3-pound shortening can or other 6- to 8-cup mold. Cover loosely with aluminum foil. Place in slow cooker. Cover and cook on high 2 to 3 hours or until a skewer inserted into bread comes out clean.

Cool in mold 10 to 20 minutes. Invert and cool on wire rack. Cool completely before slicing.

round whole-wheat sandwich bread

Begin this at 9 o'clock in the morning and serve it for lunch. Perfect for round lunch-meat slices. Bread rises and cooks in the slow cooker.

Yield: 1 loaf

1 package active dry yeast
1 cup warm water (105–115°F)
1 tablespoon sugar
2 tablespoons vegetable oil

1½ cups whole-wheat flour
1½ cups all-purpose flour
1 teaspoon salt

Dissolve yeast in warm water in a large bowl. Add sugar, oil, and whole-wheat flour. Stir vigorously until smooth. Cover and let stand in a warm place for ½ hour.

Stir in all-purpose flour and salt. Knead on a lightly floured surface 1 to 2 minutes, until smooth. Pat into a greased 48-ounce fruit-juice can trimmed (see front of book) to barely fit under the lid of the covered slow cooker.

Place can in slow cooker. Cover and cook on high about 2 hours, until a skewer inserted into the loaf comes out clean.

Allow loaf to cool in can about ½ hour. Invert and shake gently to loosen. Cool on a wire rack. Serve while warm. Loaf will rise and touch lid during cooking; do not take lid off until loaf has cooked the full 2 hours.

round pumpernickel sandwich bread

Another bread well-suited for use with round luncheon meats.

Yield: 1 loaf

1 package active dry yeast	2 tablespoons vegetable oil
¾ cup lukewarm water	1¼ cups all-purpose flour
2 tablespoons molasses	1¼ cups rye flour
1¼ teaspoons salt	1 tablespoon caraway seeds

Dissolve yeast in warm water in a large bowl. Add molasses, salt, oil, and the all-purpose flour. Stir vigorously until smooth. Cover and let stand in a warm place for ½ hour.

Stir in the rye flour and caraway seeds. Knead on a lightly floured surface about 2 minutes, until smooth. Pat into a greased 48-ounce fruit-juice can trimmed to barely fit under the lid of the covered slow cooker (see front of book).

Place can in slow cooker. Cover and cook on high about 2 hours, until a skewer inserted into the loaf comes out clean.

Allow loaf to cool in can about ½ hour. Invert and shake gently to loosen loaf. Cool on a wire rack. Slice when cool.

apricot–nut bread

Yield: 1 round loaf

½ cup chopped dried apricots
½ cup water
1 egg
2 tablespoons vegetable oil
1 cup sugar
½ cup orange juice
¾ teaspoon salt
1 cup walnuts, chopped
2 cups sifted all-purpose flour
3 teaspoons baking powder
¼ teaspoon baking soda

Soak apricots in the water for 30 minutes.

Combine egg, oil, sugar, orange juice, and salt. Beat until light and fluffy. Stir in apricot–water mixture and nuts.

Sift together the flour, baking powder, and soda. Stir into the beaten mixture only until well-blended.

Pour into a greased 7- or 8-cup mold or 3-pound shortening can. Cover loosely with aluminum foil. Place in slow cooker and cook on high 2 to 3 hours or until a long skewer inserted into bread comes out clean.

Cool 10 to 20 minutes in can and invert on a wire rack. Cool completely before slicing.

pumpkin tea bread

This bread is quite moist and delicate when baked in the slow cooker. Nice to pack for lunches.

Yield: 1 round loaf

1 cup sugar
½ cup butter
2 eggs
¾ teaspoon cinnamon
½ teaspoon nutmeg
½ teaspoon cloves
½ teaspoon salt
1 cup pureed cooked pumpkin (canned may be used)
2 cups sifted all-purpose flour
1½ teaspoons baking powder
½ teaspoon baking soda

Combine sugar, butter, eggs, spices, and salt. Beat until light and fluffy. Add pumpkin and beat only until combined

Sift together the flour, baking powder, and baking soda. Stir into the beaten mixture.

Pour into a greased 3-pound shortening can or other 7- to 8-cup mold. Cover loosely with aluminum foil. Place in slow cooker. Cover and cook on high 2 to 3 hours or until a long skewer inserted into bread comes out clean.

Cool 10 to 20 minutes, then invert mold on a rack. Slice and serve with whipped cream.

desserts

baked apples with cranberry sauce

Yield: 4 servings

4 large apples, cored but not through the bottom
8 tablespoons whole cranberry sauce
1 tablespoon butter
4 tablespoons sugar

Fill the cored apples with cranberry sauce. Dot with butter. Place in slow cooker, not touching the sides. Stack, if necessary. Cover and cook on low 3 to 4 hours.

Remove to small dishes. Serve hot or cold. Sprinkle with sugar just before serving.

baked apples with cranberry sauce

apples baked in wine with rum

Yield: 6 servings

    2 tablespoons chopped walnuts
    2 tablespoons chopped dates
    1 tablespoon chopped candied cherries
    2 tablespoons confectioners' sugar
    **6 large apples, cored but not through the
        bottom**
    1 cup dry white wine
    3 tablespoons rum
    Whipped cream for a garnish

*apples baked in
wine with rum*

Combine walnuts, dates, cherries, and sugar. Fill the cored apples with the mixture. Arrange filled apples in the slow cooker, not touching the sides, where they may burn. Apples may be stacked upon one another if staggered. Pour wine around apples. Cover and cook on low 3 to 4 hours.

Remove to dessert dishes and ladle the wine and accumulated cooking juices around each. Pour rum over fillings and garnish with whipped cream.

baked apples with assorted fillings

Yield: 6 apples

    6 apples, cored but not through the bottom
    Brown sugar and cinnamon
    Raisins
    Honey

Stuff the cored apples with either the raisins, brown sugar, or honey. Arrange in the slow cooker, not touching the sides, where they may burn. Apples may be stacked if staggered in layers. Water is not necessary unless you wish to add about ½ cup to serve with the apples when they are done. Cook on low 3 to 4 hours, until soft. Serve hot or chilled.

flaming baked apples

Yield: 4 servings

2 tablespoons chopped candied ginger (or candied orange peel or other candied fruit)
2 tablespoons raisins
4 large apples, cored but not through the bottom
2 to 4 tablespoons sugar
¼ cup warm plum brandy or vodka for flaming

Combine the candied ginger and raisins and place inside the cored apples. Arrange filled apples in the slow cooker, not touching the sides, where they may burn. Sprinkle with sugar. Cover and cook on low 3 to 4 hours.

When done, remove, and pour warmed brandy or vodka over apples. Ignite, and serve while still flaming.

flaming baked apples

apple slump

A favorite recipe of Louisa May Alcott, author of *Little Women*, is adapted here for your slow cooker. She was so fond of this dessert, she named her Concord, Massachusetts home, Apple Slump, after it. You'll find it to be a hearty fruit dessert.

Yield: 4 or 5 servings

6 cups apple slices
½ cup sugar
1 teaspoon cinnamon
½ cup water

dumplings

1 cup sifted all-purpose flour
1½ teaspoons baking powder
½ teaspoon salt
2 tablespoons butter or margarine
½ cup milk

nutmeg sauce

Scant ½ cup sugar
½ tablespoon all-purpose flour
½ cup water
½ tablespoon butter
½ teaspoon nutmeg

Place apples, sugar, cinnamon, and water in slow cooker. Cover and cook on low 4 to 6 hours, until apples are tender. Turn heat on high and prepare dumplings.

To prepare dumplings, sift together the flour, baking powder, and salt. Cut in butter; stir in the milk. Drop from a tablespoon on top of hot apples. Cover and continue to cook on high for about 30 minutes without removing the lid.

Meanwhile, prepare Nutmeg Sauce. Combine sugar and flour in a saucepan. Stir in water; bring to a boil, stirring constantly until thickened. Stir in butter and nutmeg.

Place hot apples and dumplings in dessert bowls and spoon hot Nutmeg Sauce over each.

pears in wine

Yield: 6 servings

6 pears, cored and halved lengthwise
¾ cup brown sugar
1 cup dry red wine
4 lemon slices
4 whole cloves
1 stick cinnamon
Sweetened heavy cream, whipped

Place pears in slow cooker. Combine sugar, wine, lemon, and spices. Pour over pears. Cover and cook on low for 3 to 4 hours. Cool and serve with whipped cream.

stewed plums

Yield: 8 servings

3 pounds plums
Water
4 whole cloves
1 stick cinnamon

Outer peel of 1 lemon
Sugar to taste
Sour cream

Wash plums and poke a few holes into each with a toothpick. Place in slow cooker. Add water to half the depth of the fruit. Add cloves, cinnamon, and lemon peel. Cover and cook on low 3 to 4 hours or until tender. Add sugar to sweeten.

Serve warm or cold with a dollop of sour cream.

stewed plums

fruits and honey dessert

Yield: 4 servings

**2 peaches, peeled and cubed
2 cups fresh or frozen pineapple cubes
2 apples, peeled, cored, and cut into rings
1¼ cups water or pineapple juice
¼ cup honey
2 lemon slices
1 stick cinnamon
1 banana, sliced lengthwise then in half
2 tablespoons sliced blanched almonds
½ cup heavy cream, whipped
4 cherries**

Combine all but the last 4 ingredients in the slow cooker. Cover and cook on low about 2 or 3 hours. Add banana. Divide into 4 portions.
Serve warm, garnished with almonds, whipped cream, and cherries.

fruits and honey dessert

mixed stewed fruit

A fruit compote with a light, delicately spiced, slightly sweet, citrus-flavored sauce.

Yield: 4 to 6 servings

1 11-ounce package mixed
    dried fruits
2 apples, peeled, cored, and sliced
    into ½-inch-thick rings
⅓ cup raisins, golden preferred

2 lemon slices
¼ cup orange juice
¼ cup sugar
1 stick cinnamon
2 cups water

Combine all ingredients in the slow cooker. Cover and cook on low 2 to 3 hours. Serve warm or chilled.

Variations

Soft fruits such as sliced bananas, canned pineapple, fresh strawberries, or seedless grapes can be added just before serving.

jolly madame

A dessert that is a little different—not quite a pudding, not really a cake.

Yield: 4 small servings

4 egg yolks
¼ cup sugar
Pinch salt
Fresh bread crumbs from
    3 slices bread

4 egg whites
½ cup heavy cream
2 tablespoons brown sugar
2 tablespoons finely
    chopped almonds

Beat yolks, sugar, and salt together in a small bowl until light and lemon-colored. Add bread crumbs.

Beat egg whites until stiff.

Whip cream.

Fold yolk-crumb-sugar mixture, beaten whites, and whipped cream together.

Butter a 4-cup mold; sprinkle with brown sugar and almonds. Fill with prepared batter and cover tightly with aluminum foil.

Place mold on a trivet in the slow cooker. Add boiling water to come halfway up sides of mold. Cover and cook on high 1 hour.

Remove mold, cool, and invert to remove pudding. Serve with Caramel Sauce.

caramel sauce

3 tablespoons sugar
6 tablespoons water

Melt and brown sugar over low heat in a skillet. Add water, bring to a rapid boil, remove from heat, and pour at once over pudding.

zwieback pudding

Yield: 4 servings

¼ cup butter
¼ cup sugar
4 egg yolks
10 pieces zwieback (4 ounces),
    crushed to fine crumbs
3 ounces ground almonds

½ cup raisins
Grated rind of lemon
1 cup milk
½ teaspoon salt
4 egg whites
2 tablespoons bread crumbs

Cream butter and sugar; gradually beat in yolks until mixture is light. Blend in zwieback crumbs, almonds, raisins, lemon peel, milk, and salt.

In a separate bowl, beat egg whites until stiff. Carefully fold into egg-yolk mixture. Pour into a 1-quart mold that has been buttered and sprinkled with bread crumbs. Cover mold with aluminum foil and place on a trivet in the slow cooker. Add boiling water to come about halfway up the sides of the mold. Cover and cook on high about 1 hour or until a toothpick inserted into pudding comes out clean.

Remove mold, let rest for 5 minutes, then turn out onto a platter. Serve warm.

english plum pudding

A traditional holiday dessert, rich and fragrant, served with a favorite sauce.

Yield: 6 servings

1 cup raisins
1½ cups currants (or raisins
    if currants are unavailable)
½ cup chopped mixed candied fruit
    (citron, orange peel, lemon peel)
½ cup chopped almonds or walnuts
2 cups soft bread crumbs
¾ cup brown sugar

½ teaspoon nutmeg
½ teaspoon cinnamon
Dash ginger
2 ounces chopped or ground suet
⅓ cup milk
1 egg
3 tablespoons orange juice or
    4 tablespoons brandy

Combine all ingredients and mix well. Pack into a well-greased 1-quart mold. Cover with aluminum foil and fasten on with string. Place mold on a trivet in the slow cooker and add about 3 inches of boiling water. Cover and cook on high 5 to 6 hours.

Remove mold and let stand 15 minutes. Loosen pudding with a knife around edges. Unmold and serve with Hard Sauce (recipes follow).

Pudding may be cooled at room temperature in mold, refrigerated, and rewarmed by steaming in slow cooker for an hour before serving.

Picture on previous page: zwieback pudding

assorted hard sauces for plum pudding

orange hard sauce

Yield: ½ cup

> **1 cup confectioners' sugar**
> **¼ cup soft butter or margarine**
> **1 tablespoon orange juice**
> **1 teaspoon grated orange rind**

Combine all ingredients and beat until light. Serve chilled or at room temperature with steamed pudding.

brandy hard sauce

Substitute 1 tablespoon brandy for the orange juice and rind.

lemon hard sauce

Substitute lemon juice and rind for the orange juice and rind.

mocha hard sauce

Substitute 2 tablespoons strong coffee and 2 teaspoons cocoa for the rind and 1 tablespoon milk for the orange juice.

blueberry hard sauce

Beat in ½ cup blueberries, a few at a time. Omit orange juice and rind.

pink cinnamon–vanilla custard

A quick and nourishing dessert. The slow cooker is used here in place of your oven.

Yield: 4 servings

> **2 cups milk**
> **¼ cup sugar**
> **2 eggs**
> **1 teaspoon vanilla**
> **Generous dash cinnamon**
> **Few drops red food coloring**

Whisk together all ingredients in a 1-quart mold until well-blended. Cover mold with aluminum foil and set on a trivet in the slow cooker. Add boiling water to a depth of about 1 inch. Cover and cook on high about 1¼ hours or until a knife inserted 1 inch from the mold sides comes out clean.

Serve warm or chilled. Serve alone or spooned over sliced fresh fruit. Do not overcook, or the network of egg and milk proteins will contract and water will separate out.

honey–vanilla custard

Yield: 4 servings

Omit cinnamon and use ⅓ cup honey in place of ¼ cup sugar in preceding recipe.

coffee copenhagen

Yield: 8 servings

8 cups hot coffee
1 cup rum
¾ cup sugar
2 sticks cinnamon or 1 teaspoon ground cinnamon
12 whole cloves

Combine all ingredients in slow cooker. Cover and keep warm on low for up to 2 hours. Ladle into mugs or tall, heavy glasses.

coffee copenhagen

spiced tea

Yield: 6 cups

5 cups boiling water
5 tea bags
¾ cup sugar
¼ cup strained orange juice

½ cup strained lemon juice
6 cloves
1 stick cinnamon

Pour boiling water over tea bags in slow cooker; let steep 1 to 2 minutes. Remove tea bags. Add remaining ingredients, cover, and hold on low for 2 to 3 hours.

Ladle directly from the crock pot into warm cups. Tea may be garnished with thin orange or lemon slices.

tea punch

Yield: About 8 cups

3 cups strong black tea
3 cups dry red wine
¾ cup orange juice
1 cup rum
3 whole cloves
1 stick cinnamon
¾ cup sugar
6 to 8 lemon slices as a garnish

Combine all ingredients except lemon slices in slow cooker. Cover and hold on low 2 to 3 hours.

Ladle hot into mugs. Garnish with lemon slices.

hot fruit punch

Yield: About 2 quarts

3 cups orange juice
1 quart cranberry juice
1 12-ounce can light beer
2 apples, cored, peeled, and sliced
    thin

½ cup brown sugar
1 stick cinnamon
½ teaspoon ginger
½ teaspoon nutmeg
4 slices orange as a garnish

Combine all ingredients except orange slices in slow cooker. Cover and cook on low 1 hour. Garnish with orange slices. Serve hot.

tea punch

lamb's wool

Yield: 8 servings

8 apples, peeled, cored, and coarsely
    chopped
¼ cup butter
2 quarts beer or ale
1 cup sugar
½ teaspoon nutmeg
½ teaspoon ginger

lamb's wool

Combine all ingredients in slow cooker. Cover and cook on low 2 to 3 hours.
Remove apples, mash or sieve, and return to beer mixture. Serve very hot from
slow cooker.

137

mulled cider

Yield: 2 quarts

2 quarts cider
1 orange, sliced
1 lemon, sliced
2 sticks cinnamon
8 whole cloves

Combine all ingredients in slow cooker. Cover and heat on low for 1 hour. Ladle into punch cups.

hot cider cocktail

Yield: 6 cups

4 cups water
1 cup rum
⅓ cup curaçao
Sugar to taste
4 whole cloves
Lemon slices for garnish

hot cider cocktail

Combine all ingredients except lemon slices in slow cooker. Cover and heat on low 2 to 3 hours.
Ladle hot into mugs. Garnish with lemon slices.

swedish glogg

Yield: About 2 quarts

> 1 bottle port (4/5 quart)
> 1 bottle claret (4/5 quart)
> ½ cup apricot brandy
> ½ cup raisins or currants
> 6 dried apricot halves, chopped
> 12 blanched almonds
> 4 whole cloves
> 2 sticks cinnamon
> 4 whole cardamom

Combine all ingredients in the slow cooker. Cover and cook on low for 1 to 2 hours. Serve hot.

wassail bowl

Yield: About 2 quarts

> 2 cups sugar
> 1 teaspoon nutmeg
> 1 teaspoon ginger
> ½ teaspoon mace
> 8 whole cloves
> 8 whole allspice
> 1 stick cinnamon
> 2 quarts dry sherry
> 6 eggs, separated
> ½ cup brandy

Combine sugar, spices, and sherry in slow cooker. Cover and cook on low for 1 hour, stirring occasionally. Whisk in the egg yolks and brandy.

Beat the egg whites until soft peaks form. Fold into the sherry mixture. Serve warm. Do not allow the mixture to boil, or the eggs will curdle.

snacks

party snack

This is a long-time favorite at cocktail parties. Usually toasted in the oven, it can be prepared with less electricity in your slow cooker.

Yield: About 6 cups

⅔ cup butter or margarine, melted
1¼ teaspoons garlic salt or celery salt
1½ tablespoons Worcestershire sauce
3 cups Wheat Chex
3 cups Rice Chex
¾ cup unsalted nuts

Combine all ingredients in the slow cooker. Cover and heat on low 3 to 4 hours with lid slightly ajar. Stir occasionally.
Serve warm from the pot or cool and store in airtight jars.

curry party snack

Yield: 4 cups

⅓ cup butter or margarine
½ teaspoon curry powder
¾ teaspoon salt
4 cups Rice Chex
½ cup almonds

Combine all ingredients in the slow cooker. Cover and heat on low 3 to 4 hours with lid slightly ajar. Stir occasionally.
Serve warm from the pot, or cool and store in airtight jars.

mexican caramel candy (cajeta)

Yield: Varies with use

1 14-ounce can sweetened condensed milk, unopened, label removed

Place unopened can condensed milk in the slow cooker. Add hot water to cover. Cover and cook on high for 3 hours. Remove can and chill.

Spoon candied milk into a serving dish. Serve with crackers, unsalted preferred. Or serve over ice cream, gelatin desserts, or alone in small dishes with a demitasse spoon.

Cajeta means "small box." The candy is sold in small wooden boxes with small spoons from Mexican street corners.

index

142

144